what's cooking
chicken

Tom Bridge

p

This is a Parragon Publishing book
First published in 2004

Parragon Publishing
Queen Street House
4 Queen Street
Bath BA1 1HE
United Kingdom

Copyright © Parragon 2004

ISBN: 1-40542-537-7

Printed in China

ACKNOWLEDGMENTS
PHOTOGRAPHY: St John Asprey

NOTE

This book uses imperial, metric, or US cup measurements. Follow the same units of measurement throughout;
do not mix imperial and metric. All spoon measurements are level: teaspoons are assumed to be 5 ml
and tablespoons are assumed to be 15 ml. Unless otherwise stated, milk is assumed to be whole, eggs and
individual vegetables such as potatoes are medium, and pepper is freshly ground black pepper.

The times given for each recipe are an approximate guide only. The preparation times may differ according to
the techniques used by different people and the cooking times may vary as a result of the type of oven used.
Ovens should be preheated to the specified temperature. If using a fan-assisted oven, check the manufacturer's
instructions for adjusting the time and temperature. The preparation times include chilling
and marinating times, where appropriate.

Recipes using raw or very lightly cooked eggs should be avoided by infants, the elderly,
pregnant women, convalescents, and anyone suffering from an illness.

contents

introduction

Chicken has become justly popular around the world and plays an important part in the modern diet, being reasonably priced and nutritionally sound. A versatile meat, it lends itself to an enormous range of cooking methods and cuisines. Its unassertive flavor means that it is equally suited to cooking with both sweet and savory flavors. Because it has a low fat content, especially without the skin, it is an ideal meat for low-cholesterol and calorie-controlled diets. As well as being an excellent source of protein, chicken contains valuable minerals, such as potassium and phosphorus, and some of the B vitamins.

COOKING METHODS FOR CHICKEN

ROASTING Remove any fat from the body cavity. Rinse the bird inside and out with water, then pat dry with paper towels. Season the cavity generously with salt and pepper and add stuffing, herbs, or lemon if wished. Spread the breast of the chicken with softened butter or oil. Set on a rack in a roasting pan or shallow baking dish. Roast the bird, basting two or three times with the pan drippings during roasting. If the chicken is browning too quickly, cover it with foil. Test for doneness by using a meat thermometer or insert a skewer into the thickest part of the thigh. If the chicken is cooked, the juices will run clear with no trace of pink. Place the bird on a carving board and let rest for at least 15 minutes before serving. Make a sauce or gravy from the drippings in the roasting pan.

BROILING The intense heat of the broiler quickly seals the succulent flesh beneath a crisp, golden exterior. Place the chicken 4–6 inches/10–15 cm away from a medium heat source. If the chicken seems to be browning too quickly, reduce the heat slightly. If the chicken is broiled at too high a temperature too near to the heat, the outside will burn before the inside is cooked. If it is cooked for too long under low heat, it will dry out. Divide the chicken into parts to ensure even cooking. Breast meat, if cooked in one piece, can be rather dry, so it is best to cut it into chunks for kabobs. Wings are best for speedy broiling.

FRYING This is suitable for small thighs, drumsticks, and parts. Dry the chicken pieces with paper towels so that they brown properly and to prevent them spitting during cooking. The chicken can be coated in seasoned flour, egg, and bread crumbs or a batter. Heat oil or a mixture of oil and butter in a heavy-bottomed skillet. When very hot, add the chicken pieces, skin-side down. Fry until they are deep golden brown all over, turning the pieces frequently during cooking. Drain well on paper towels before serving.

SAUTÉEING This is ideal for small pieces or small birds such as squab chickens. Heat a little oil or a mixture of oil and butter in a heavy-bottomed skillet. Add the chicken and fry over medium heat until golden brown, turning frequently. Add stock or other liquid, bring to a boil, then cover and reduce the heat. Cook gently until the chicken is cooked through.

STIR-FRYING Skinless, boneless chicken is cut into small pieces of equal size to ensure that the meat cooks evenly and stays succulent. Preheat a wok or pan before adding a small amount of oil. When the oil begins to smoke, add the chicken and stir-fry with your chosen flavorings for 3–4 minutes, or until cooked through. Other ingredients can be cooked at the same time, or the chicken can be cooked by itself,

then removed from the wok or pan while you stir-fry the remaining ingredients. Return the chicken to the wok once the other ingredients are cooked.

CASSEROLING This is good for cooking parts from larger, more mature chickens, although smaller chickens can be cooked whole. The slow cooking produces tender meat with a good flavor. Brown the chicken in butter or oil or a mixture of both. Add some stock, wine, or a mixture of both together with seasonings and herbs, cover, and cook on the stove or in the oven until the chicken is tender. Add a selection of lightly sautéed vegetables to the casserole about halfway through the cooking time.

BRAISING This is a method that does not require liquid. The chicken pieces or a small whole chicken and vegetables are cooked together slowly in a low oven. Heat some oil in an ovenproof, flameproof casserole and gently fry the chicken until golden. Remove the chicken and fry a selection of vegetables until they are almost tender. Replace the chicken, cover tightly, and cook very gently on the stove or in a low oven until the chicken and vegetables are tender.

POACHING This is a gentle cooking method that produces tender chicken and a stock that can be used to make a sauce to serve with the chicken. Place a whole chicken, a bouquet garni envelope, a leek, a carrot, and an onion in a large, flameproof casserole. Cover with water, season to taste with salt and pepper, and bring to a boil. Cover and simmer for 1½–2 hours, or until the chicken is tender. Lift the chicken out, remove and discard the bouquet garni, and use the stock to make a sauce. The vegetables can be blended and used to thicken the stock, then served with the chicken.

FOOD SAFETY & TIPS

Chicken is liable to be contaminated by salmonella bacteria, which can cause severe food poisoning. When storing, handling, and preparing poultry, certain precautions must be observed to prevent the possibility of food poisoning.

• Check the sell-by date and best-before dates. After buying, take the chicken home in a freezer bag.

• Return frozen birds immediately to the freezer.

• If storing in the refrigerator, remove the wrappings and store any giblets separately. Place the chicken in a shallow dish to catch drips. Cover and chill on the bottom shelf for 2–3 days, depending on the best-before date. Avoid contact between raw chicken and cooked food during storage and preparation. Wash your hands after handling raw chicken.

• Prepare raw chicken on a cutting board that can be easily cleaned and bleached.

• Frozen birds should be thawed before cooking. If time permits, thaw for 36 hours in the refrigerator, or thaw for 12 hours in a cool place. Bacteria breed in warm food at room temperature and when chicken is thawing. Cooking at high temperatures kills bacteria. There should be no ice crystals and the flesh should feel flexible. Cook as soon as possible after thawing.

• Make sure chicken is thoroughly cooked. Test for doneness using a meat thermometer—the thigh should reach at least 175°F/79°C when cooked—or pierce the thickest part of a thigh with a skewer; the juices should run clear, not pink. Never partially cook chicken with the intention of completing cooking later.

CHICKEN STOCK

Chicken stock is usually made from a whole bird or wings, backs, and legs. However, it can be made using chicken bones and the carcass cooked with vegetables and flavorings. Homemade stock can be stored in the freezer for up to 6 months.

To make chicken stock, add the wings, backs, or whole chicken to a pan with 2 quartered onions. Cook until the chicken and onion are browned. Cover with water, bring to a boil, and skim off any scum that rises to the surface. Add 2 chopped carrots, 2 chopped celery stalks, a bunch of fresh parsley, a few bay leaves, 1 fresh thyme sprig, and a few peppercorns. Simmer for 3 hours. Strain into a bowl. Cool, then chill. When cold, remove the fat from the surface.

soups & snacks

Chicken soup has a long tradition of being comforting and good for us, and some cultures even think of it as a cure for all ills. It is certainly satisfying, full of flavor, and easy to digest. For the best results, use a good homemade chicken stock, although when time is at a premium, a good-quality bouillon cube can be used instead. Every cuisine in the world has its own favorite version of chicken soup and in this section you'll find a selection of recipes from as far afield as Scotland, Italy, and China.

As chicken is so versatile and quick to cook, it is perfect for innovative and appetizing snacks. Its unassertive flavor means that it can be enlivened by exotic fruits and spices and other ingredients, such as mirin, sesame oil, and fresh gingerroot. There are fritters, salads, and drumsticks that are stuffed and baked, or served with delicious fruity salsas. Because chicken pieces travel well and are easy to eat, many of the recipes are ideal to take on picnics or to pack into a lunch box.

cream of chicken & lemon soup

serves 4

20 minutes

I hour 20 minutes

4 tbsp butter
8 shallots, thinly sliced
2 carrots, thinly sliced
2 celery stalks, thinly sliced
9 oz/250 g skinless, boneless
   chicken breast, finely chopped
3 lemons

5 cups Chicken Stock
   (see page 5)
salt and pepper
2/3 cup heavy cream

to garnish
fresh parsley sprigs
lemon slices

This refreshing soup with its tangy lemon flavor is perfect on summer days.

Melt the butter in a large, heavy-bottomed pan. Add the vegetables and chicken and cook gently for 8 minutes.

Thinly pare the lemons and blanch the lemon rind in boiling water for 3 minutes.

Squeeze the juice from the lemons.

Add the lemon rind and freshly squeezed lemon juice to the pan with the stock.

Bring slowly to a boil, then simmer for 50 minutes. Let the soup cool, then transfer to a food processor or blender and process until smooth. Return the soup to the pan, re-heat, season to taste with salt and pepper, then add the cream. Do not boil at this stage, or the soup will curdle.

Transfer the soup to a tureen or warm individual bowls. Garnish with parsley sprigs and lemon slices and serve.

variation

For an alternative citrus flavor, use 4 oranges in place of the lemons.

tom's chicken soup

serves 4

10 minutes

1 hour 10 minutes

3 rindless smoked lean bacon strips, chopped

1 lb 2 oz/500 g boneless chicken, chopped

2 tbsp butter

3 potatoes, chopped

3 onions, chopped

2$\frac{1}{2}$ cups giblet or Chicken Stock (see page 5)

salt and pepper

2$\frac{1}{2}$ cups milk

$\frac{2}{3}$ cup heavy cream

2 tbsp chopped fresh parsley

Irish soda bread, to serve

The potato has been part of the Irish diet for centuries. This recipe is originally from the north of Ireland, in the beautiful area of Moira, County Down.

Gently fry the chopped bacon and chicken without any fat in a large, heavy-bottomed pan for 10 minutes. Add the butter, potatoes, and onions and cook for 15 minutes, stirring constantly.

Add the stock and milk, then bring the soup to a boil. Reduce the heat and simmer for 45 minutes. Season to taste with salt and pepper.

Blend in the cream and simmer for 5 minutes. Stir in the chopped fresh parsley, then transfer the soup to a warm tureen or individual bowls and serve with soda bread.

cook's tip

Soda bread is not made with yeast as bread usually is. Instead, it is made with baking soda as the raising agent. It can be made with all-purpose or whole-wheat flour.

variation

For a more filling, main course soup, you can add any number of different vegetables, for example leeks, celery root, or even corn.

chicken & leek soup

serves·6

10 minutes

1 hour 15 minutes

12 oz/350 g boneless chicken
12 oz/350 g leeks
2 tbsp butter
5 cups Chicken Stock
  (see page 5)

1 bouquet garni envelope
salt and white pepper
8 pitted prunes, halved
cooked rice and diced bell peppers
  (optional)

This satisfying soup can be served as an entrée. You can add rice and bell peppers to make it even more hearty, as well as colorful.

cook's tip

If you have time, make the chicken stock yourself, using the recipe on page 5. Alternatively, you can buy good fresh stock from supermarkets.

Instead of the bouquet garni, you can use a bunch of fresh, mixed herbs, tied together with string. Choose herbs such as parsley, thyme, and rosemary.

Using a sharp knife, cut the chicken and leeks into 1-inch/2.5-cm pieces.

Melt the butter in a large, heavy-bottomed pan. Add the chicken and leeks and fry for 8 minutes, stirring occasionally.

Add the stock and bouquet garni to the mixture in the pan, and season to taste with salt and pepper.

Bring the soup to a boil, then simmer over low heat for 45 minutes.

Add the prunes with some cooked rice and diced bell peppers (if using), and simmer for 20 minutes. Remove and discard the bouquet garni. Pour the soup into a warm tureen or individual bowls and serve.

thai chicken noodle

soup

serves 4–6

10 minutes

20 minutes

1 sheet dried egg noodles from a
 9 oz/250 g pack

1 tbsp corn oil

4 skinless, boneless chicken
 thighs, diced

1 bunch of scallions, sliced

2 garlic cloves, chopped

3/4-inch/2-cm piece fresh gingerroot,
 finely chopped

3 1/2 cups Chicken Stock
 (see page 5)

generous 3/4 cup coconut milk

3 tsp Thai red curry paste

3 tbsp peanut butter

2 tbsp light soy sauce

salt and pepper

1 small red bell pepper, seeded and
 chopped

1/2 cup frozen peas

*Quick to make, this hot and
spicy soup is hearty and
warming. If you like your food
really fiery, add a chopped dried
or fresh chile with its seeds.*

variation

*Thai green curry paste can be
used instead of the red curry
paste for a less fiery flavor.*

Place the noodles in a shallow, heatproof dish and soak in boiling water according to the package instructions.

Heat the oil in a large, heavy-bottomed pan or preheated wok. Add the chicken and stir-fry for 5 minutes, or until lightly browned. Add the white part of the scallions, the garlic, and gingerroot and stir-fry for 2 minutes.

Add the stock, coconut milk, curry paste, peanut butter, and soy sauce. Season to taste with salt and pepper. Bring to a boil, stirring constantly, then simmer for 8 minutes, stirring occasionally. Add the red bell pepper, peas, and green scallion tops and cook for an additional 2 minutes.

Add the drained noodles and heat through. Spoon into individual bowls and serve immediately.

chicken & pasta broth

serves 6

15 minutes

20 minutes

12 oz/350 g boneless chicken breasts
2 tbsp corn oil
1 onion, diced
9 oz/250 g carrots, diced
9 oz/250 g cauliflower florets
3½ cups Chicken Stock
  (see page 5)

2 tsp dried mixed herbs
4½ oz/125 g small dried pasta shapes
salt and pepper
Parmesan cheese, for sprinkling
  (optional)
crusty bread, to serve

This satisfying soup makes a good lunch or supper dish and you can use any vegetables that you have at hand. Children will love the tiny pasta shapes.

Using a sharp knife, finely dice the chicken, discarding any skin.

Heat the oil in a large, heavy-bottomed pan and quickly sauté the chicken, onions, carrots, and cauliflower until they are lightly colored.

Stir in the stock and mixed herbs. Bring to a boil and add the pasta shapes. Return to a boil, cover, and simmer for 10 minutes, stirring occasionally to prevent the pasta shapes sticking together.

Season to taste with salt and pepper and sprinkle with Parmesan cheese (if using). Serve with fresh crusty bread.

cook's tip

You can use any small pasta shapes for this soup—try conchigliette or ditalini, or even spaghetti broken up into small pieces. To make a fun soup for children, you could add animal-shaped or alphabet pasta.

variation

Broccoli florets can be used to replace the cauliflower florets. Substitute 2 tablespoons chopped fresh mixed herbs for the dried mixed herbs.

chicken consommé

serves 8–10

40 minutes, plus
30 minutes standing

20 minutes

8 cups Chicken Stock
(see page 5)
2/3 cup medium sherry
4 egg whites, plus egg shells

salt and pepper
4 oz/115 g cooked chicken,
thinly sliced

This is a very flavorful soup, especially if you make it from fresh chicken stock. Egg shells are used to give a crystal clear appearance.

cook's tip

Consommé is usually garnished with freshly cooked pasta shapes, noodles, rice, or lightly cooked vegetables. Alternatively, you could garnish it with omelet strips, drained first on paper towels.

Place the stock and sherry in a large, heavy-bottomed pan and heat gently for 5 minutes.

Add the egg whites and the egg shells to the stock and whisk until the mixture begins to boil.

Remove the pan from the heat and let the mixture subside for 10 minutes. Repeat this process 3 times. This allows the egg white to trap the sediments in the stock to clarify the soup. Let the consommé cool for 5 minutes.

Carefully place a piece of fine cheesecloth over a clean pan. Ladle the soup over the cheesecloth and strain into the pan.

Repeat this process twice, then gently re-heat the consommé. Season to taste with salt and pepper, then add the cooked chicken slices. Pour the soup into a warm serving dish or individual bowls.

Garnish with any of the suggestions in the Cook's Tip and serve.

chicken
mulligatawny soup

serves 4

15 minutes

1 hour 10 minutes

4 tbsp butter

1 onion, sliced

1 garlic clove, crushed

1 lb 2 oz/500 g boneless
  chicken, diced

2 oz/55 g rindless smoked
  bacon, diced

1 small turnip, diced

2 carrots, diced

1 small cooking apple, diced

2 tbsp mild curry powder

1 tbsp curry paste

1 tbsp tomato paste

1 tbsp all-purpose flour

5 cups Chicken Stock
  (see page 5)

salt and pepper

2/3 cup heavy cream

1 tsp chopped fresh cilantro,
  to garnish

freshly cooked rice, to serve

This spicy soup was brought to the West by army and service personnel returning from India.

cook's tip

This soup may be frozen for up to 1 month; if stored for any longer, the spices may cause it to taste musty.

Melt the butter in a large, heavy-bottomed pan. Add the onion, garlic, chicken, and bacon and cook for 5 minutes.

Add the turnip, carrots, and apple and cook for an additional 2 minutes.

Blend in the curry powder, curry paste, and tomato paste, then sprinkle over the flour.

Add the stock and bring to a boil, cover, and simmer over low heat for 1 hour.

Transfer the soup to a food processor or blender and process until smooth, then return to the rinsed-out pan and re-heat gently. Season well with salt and pepper and gradually blend in the cream. Garnish the soup with chopped cilantro and serve with freshly cooked rice.

chicken & pea soup

serves 4–6

10 minutes

2 hours 10 minutes

3 rindless smoked lean bacon strips, chopped

2 lb/900 g chicken, chopped

1 large onion, chopped

1 tbsp butter

1 lb 2 oz/500 g presoaked dried peas (see Cook's Tip)

10 cups Chicken Stock (see page 5)

salt and pepper

2/3 cup heavy cream

2 tbsp chopped fresh parsley

cheesy croûtes (see Cook's Tip), to garnish

A hearty soup that is so simple to make yet packed with flavor. You can use either whole green peas or green or yellow split peas.

Place the bacon, chicken, and onion in a large, heavy-bottomed pan with a little butter and cook over low heat for 8 minutes.

Add the peas and the stock to the pan, bring to a boil, and season lightly with salt and pepper. Cover and simmer for 2 hours.

Stir the cream into the soup, sprinkle with chopped parsley, and top with cheesy croûtes.

cook's tip

Croûtes are slices of French bread that are fried or baked, then they can be sprinkled with grated cheese and lightly toasted.

If using dried peas, soak them for several hours or overnight in a large bowl of cold water. Alternatively, bring them to a boil in a pan of cold water. Remove from the heat and let cool in the water. Drain and rinse the peas before adding them to the soup.

variation

Use 3 1/2 oz/100 g chopped ham instead of the bacon, if you prefer.

cream of chicken soup

serves 4

10 minutes, plus
30 minutes cooling

30 minutes

4 tbsp unsalted butter
1 large onion, chopped
10½ oz/300 g cooked chicken,
  finely shredded
2½ cups Chicken Stock
  (see page 5)
salt and pepper

1 tbsp chopped fresh tarragon
⅔ cup heavy cream

croutons
4 thick slices day-old bread
4 tbsp olive oil
fresh tarragon leaves, to garnish

Tarragon adds a delicate anise flavor to this tasty soup. If you can't find tarragon, use parsley for a fresh taste.

variation

If you can't find fresh tarragon, freeze-dried tarragon makes a good substitute. Light cream can be used instead of the heavy cream.

To make garlic croutons, crush 3–4 garlic cloves in a mortar with a pestle and add to the oil.

Melt the butter in a large, heavy-bottomed pan, add the onion, and fry for 3 minutes. Add the chicken to the pan with 1¼ cups of the stock.

Bring to a boil, then simmer for 20 minutes. Remove the pan from the heat and let cool, then transfer the soup to a food processor or blender and process the soup until smooth.

Add the remainder of the stock and season to taste with salt and pepper.

Add the chopped tarragon, pour the soup into a tureen or individual bowls, and add a swirl of cream.

To make the croutons, cut the bread into even-size cubes. Heat the oil in a skillet. Add the bread cubes and fry until golden brown and crisp. Drain on paper towels and reserve until required.

Garnish the soup with fresh tarragon and serve with the croutons.

chicken soup with
cilantro dumplings

serves 6–8

20 minutes

3 hours 45 minutes

2 lb/900 g boneless chicken, sliced
scant 1/2 cup all-purpose flour
salt and pepper
generous 1/2 cup butter
3 tbsp corn oil
1 large carrot, chopped
1 celery stalk, chopped
1 onion, chopped
1 small turnip, chopped
1/2 cup sherry
1 tsp dried thyme
1 bay leaf
8 cups Chicken Stock
   (see page 5)

dumplings

scant 1/2 cup self-rising flour, plus
   extra for coating
1 cup fresh bread crumbs
2 tbsp shredded suet
2 tbsp chopped fresh cilantro
2 tbsp finely grated lemon rind
salt and pepper
1 egg
milk, for binding

Use the strained vegetables and chicken to make little patties. Simply mash with a little butter, shape them into round cakes, and fry in butter or oil until golden brown.

Coat the chicken slices with the flour and season well with salt and pepper.

Melt the butter in a pan. Add the chicken pieces and fry until they are lightly browned.

Add the oil to the pan and cook the vegetables until browned. Add the sherry and the remaining ingredients except the stock.

Cook for 10 minutes, then add the stock. Simmer for 3 hours, then strain into a clean pan and let cool.

To make the dumplings, mix all the dry ingredients together in a large bowl. Add the egg and blend in thoroughly, then add enough milk to form a moist dough.

Shape into small balls and roll them in a little flour.

Cook the dumplings in lightly salted boiling water for 10 minutes.

Remove them carefully with a slotted spoon and add them to the soup. Cook for an additional 12 minutes, then serve.

dickensian chicken broth

serves 4

20 minutes, plus
24 hours standing

2 hours 55 minutes

2 oz/55 g presoaked dried peas
  (see Cook's Tip, page 22)
2 lb/900 g diced chicken, fat removed
5 cups Chicken Stock
  (see page 5)
2½ cups water
generous ¼ cup barley, washed and
  drained

salt and white pepper
1 large carrot, diced
1 small turnip, diced
1 large leek, thinly sliced
1 red onion, finely chopped

*This soup is made with
traditional Scottish ingredients.
It should be left for at least
24 hours before being re-
heated, then served with
oatmeal cakes or bread.*

Place the peas and chicken in a large, heavy-bottomed pan. Add the stock
and water and bring slowly to a boil.

Skim the stock as it boils using a slotted spoon.

When all the scum is removed, add the barley and salt and pepper to
taste and let simmer for 35 minutes.

Add the remaining ingredients and let simmer for an additional 2 hours.

Skim the surface of the soup again and let the broth stand for at least
24 hours. Re-heat, taste, and adjust the seasoning, if necessary, then serve.

cook's tip

*Use either whole-grain barley or
pearl barley. Only the outer husk is
removed from whole-grain barley
and when cooked it has a nutty
flavor and a chewy texture.*

variation

*This soup is just as delicious made with
beef or lamb. Substitute 8 oz/225 g lean
beef or lamb for the chicken. Trim any fat
from the meat and cut into thin strips
before using.*

cream of chicken & orange soup

serves 4

20 minutes

1 hour 10 minutes

4 tbsp butter
8 shallots, thinly sliced
2 carrots, thinly sliced
2 celery stalks, thinly sliced
8 oz/225 g skinless, boneless chicken breast, finely chopped
3 oranges

5 cups Chicken Stock (see page 5)
salt and white pepper
2/3 cup heavy cream

to garnish
fresh parsley sprigs
2 orange slices, halved
Irish soda bread, to serve

For a tangy flavor, lemons can be used instead of oranges, and the recipe can be adapted to make duck and orange soup.

variation

Use 2 small lemons in place of the oranges. Look for organic or unwaxed lemons when using rind.

Melt the butter in a large, heavy-bottomed pan. Add the shallots, carrots, celery, and chicken and cook gently for 8 minutes, stirring occasionally.

Using a potato peeler or sharp knife, thinly pare the oranges and blanch the rind in boiling water for 3 minutes.

Squeeze the juice from the oranges. Add the orange rind and orange juice to the pan with the stock.

Bring slowly to a boil, then simmer for 50 minutes. Remove the soup from the heat and let cool, then transfer to a food processor or blender and process until smooth.

Return the soup to the rinsed-out pan and re-heat gently. Season to taste with salt and pepper and add the cream. Do not boil at this stage, or the soup will curdle.

Transfer the soup to a serving dish or individual bowls. Garnish with parsley sprigs and halved orange slices and serve with soda bread.

chicken, guinea fowl & spaghetti soup

serves 6

20 minutes

2 hours 15 minutes

1 lb 2 oz/500 g skinless chicken, chopped

1 lb 2 oz/500 g skinless guinea fowl

2 1/2 cups Chicken Stock (see page 5)

1 small onion

6 peppercorns

1 tsp cloves

pinch of mace

2/3 cup heavy cream

2 tsp butter

2 tsp all-purpose flour

4 1/2 oz/125 g quick-cook spaghetti, broken into short lengths and cooked

2 tbsp chopped fresh parsley, to garnish

Guinea fowl has a similar texture to chicken, and although it has a milder flavor than other game, it has a slightly gamier flavor than chicken.

variation

Instead of spaghetti, use small pasta shapes such as ziti or macaroni.

Place the chicken and guinea fowl in a large, heavy-bottomed pan with the stock.

Bring to a boil and add the onion, peppercorns, cloves, and mace. Simmer gently for 2 hours, or until the stock is reduced by one-third.

Strain the soup, skim off any fat, and remove any bones from the chicken and guinea fowl.

Return the soup and meat to a clean pan. Add the cream and bring slowly to a boil.

To make a roux, melt the butter in a small pan, then stir in the flour until it has a paste-like consistency. Add to the soup, stirring until slightly thickened.

Just before serving, add the cooked spaghetti.

Transfer the soup to individual serving bowls, garnish with chopped parsley, and serve.

cream of chicken & tomato soup

serves 2

15 minutes

30 minutes

4 tbsp unsalted butter
1 large onion, chopped
1 lb 2 oz/500 g skinless, boneless chicken, very finely shredded
2½ cups Chicken Stock (see page 5)
6 tomatoes, finely chopped
pinch of baking soda

salt and pepper
1 tbsp superfine sugar
⅔ cup heavy cream
fresh basil leaves, to garnish
Croutons (see page 24), to serve

This soup is very good made with fresh tomatoes, but if you prefer, you can use canned tomatoes.

Melt the butter in a large, heavy-bottomed pan. Add the onion and shredded chicken and fry for 5 minutes.

Add 1¼ cups of the stock to the pan, with the tomatoes and baking soda. Bring the soup to a boil, then simmer for 20 minutes.

Remove the pan from the heat and let the soup cool, then transfer to a food processor or blender and process until smooth.

Return the soup to the pan, add the remaining stock, season to taste with salt and pepper, and add the sugar. Pour the soup into a tureen and add a swirl of cream. Garnish with basil and serve with Croutons.

cook's tip

For a healthier version of this soup, use light cream instead of the heavy cream and omit the sugar.

variation

For an Italian-style soup, add 1 tablespoon chopped fresh basil with the stock. Alternatively, add ½ teaspoon curry powder or chili powder to make a spicier version of this soup.

chicken won ton soup

serves 4–6

10 minutes

10 minutes

filling

12 oz/350 g ground chicken

1 tbsp soy sauce

1 tsp grated fresh gingerroot

1 garlic clove, crushed

2 tsp sherry

2 scallions, chopped

1 tsp sesame oil

1 egg white

$\frac{1}{2}$ tsp cornstarch

$\frac{1}{2}$ tsp sugar

about 35 won ton wrappers

soup

6 cups Chicken Stock
  (see page 5)

1 tbsp light soy sauce

1 scallion, shredded

1 small carrot, very thinly sliced

This Chinese-style soup is delicious as an appetizer for an Asian meal or as a light meal.

Mix all the ingredients together for the filling.

Place a small spoonful of the filling in the center of each won ton wrapper.

Dampen the edges and gather up the won ton wrapper to form a pouch, enclosing the filling.

Cook the filled won tons in a pan of boiling water for 1 minute, or until they float to the top. Remove with a slotted spoon.

Bring the stock to a boil in a large pan. Add the soy sauce, scallion, carrot, and won tons to the soup. Simmer gently for 2 minutes, then serve.

cook's tip

Look for won ton wrappers in Chinese or Asian markets. Fresh wrappers can be found in the chilled compartment and they can be frozen if you wish. Wrap in plastic wrap before freezing.

variation

Substitute ground pork for the chicken.

chicken & cheese jackets

serves 4

10 minutes

50 minutes–1 hour

4 large baking potatoes
9 oz/250 g cooked, boneless
  chicken breasts
4 scallions

generous 1 cup lowfat soft cheese
  or Quark
pepper
coleslaw, green salad, or a mixed
  salad, to serve

Use the breasts from a roasted chicken for this delicious, healthy snack. Served with a mixed salad, it is an ideal light meal for a summer's day.

Preheat the oven to 400°F/200°C. Prick the potatoes all over with a fork. Bake in the preheated oven for 50 minutes, or until tender. Alternatively, cook in a microwave on High for 12–15 minutes.

Using a sharp knife, dice the chicken, trim and thickly slice the scallions, and mix with the lowfat soft cheese or Quark.

Cut a cross through the top of each potato and pull slightly apart. Spoon the chicken filling into the potatoes and sprinkle with pepper to taste. Serve with coleslaw, green salad, or a mixed salad.

cook's tip

Look for Quark in the chilled section. It is a lowfat, white, fresh curd cheese made from cow's milk with a delicate, slightly sour flavor.

variation

For another delicious filling, fry 9 oz/250 g white mushrooms in a little butter. Mix with the chicken, then add 2/3 cup plain yogurt, 1 tablespoon tomato paste, and 2 teaspoons mild curry powder. Blend well and use to fill the potatoes.

sticky chicken drummers

serves 4

20 minutes

40–50 minutes

8 skinless chicken drumsticks
3 tbsp mango chutney
2 tsp Dijon mustard
2 tsp corn oil
I tsp paprika
I tsp black mustard seeds, coarsely crushed
1/2 tsp ground turmeric
2 garlic cloves, chopped
salt and pepper

salsa
I mango, diced
I tomato, finely chopped
1/2 red onion, thinly sliced
2 tbsp chopped fresh cilantro
salt and pepper

Delicious served hot or cold, and any leftover chicken can be packed in lunch boxes for a tasty alternative to sandwiches.

variation

Use mild curry powder instead of the turmeric.

Preheat the oven to 400°F/200°C. Using a small, sharp knife, slash each drumstick 3–4 times, then place in a roasting pan.

Mix the mango chutney, mustard, oil, spices, garlic, and salt and pepper to taste together in a small bowl. Spoon over the chicken drumsticks, turning until they are coated all over with the glaze.

Bake in the preheated oven for 40 minutes, brushing with the glaze several times during cooking, until the chicken is well browned and tender and the juices run clear when a skewer is inserted into the thickest part of the meat.

To make the salsa, mix all the ingredients together in a small bowl. Season to taste with salt and pepper and let chill in the refrigerator until required.

Arrange the chicken drumsticks on a serving plate and serve hot or cold with the mango salsa.

open chicken sandwiches

serves 6

20 minutes

–

6 thick slices bread or a large French baguette cut lengthwise, then cut into 6 pieces, buttered

3 hard-cooked eggs, the yolk strained and the white chopped

2 tbsp butter, softened

2 tbsp English mustard

1 tsp anchovy essence

pepper

2¼ cups grated Cheddar cheese

3 cooked, skinless chicken breasts, finely chopped

12 slices each tomato and cucumber

These tasty sandwiches are good as a snack on their own or they can be served as part of a picnic spread.

Remove the crusts from the bread, if you like.

Reserve the yolk and the white separately from 1 egg.

Mix the remaining eggs with the softened butter, mustard, and anchovy essence in a large bowl. Season well with pepper.

Mix in the grated cheese and chopped chicken and spread the mixture on the bread.

Make alternate rows of the reserved egg yolk and the egg white on top of the chicken mixture. Arrange the tomato and cucumber slices on top of the egg and serve.

cook's tip

To soften butter, let stand at room temperature for 30 minutes or, if you are short of time, cream it in a bowl with a fork. Alternatively, there are now varieties of soft butter available from supermarkets.

variation

Add 1¾ oz/50 g finely chopped broiled bacon to the chicken and cheese mixture for a crunchier texture.

chicken pepperonata

serves 4

20 minutes

40 minutes

8 chicken thighs
2 tbsp whole-wheat flour
2 tbsp olive oil
1 small onion, thinly sliced
1 garlic clove, crushed
1 each large red, yellow, and green bell peppers, seeded and thinly sliced

14 oz/400 g canned chopped tomatoes
1 tbsp chopped fresh oregano, plus extra to garnish
salt and pepper
crusty whole-wheat bread, to serve

All the sunshine colors and flavors of the Mediterranean are combined in this easy dish.

cook's tip

If you do not have fresh oregano, use canned tomatoes with herbs already added.

For extra flavor, halve the bell peppers and broil under a preheated broiler until the skins are charred. Let cool, then remove the skins and seeds. Slice the bell peppers thinly and use in the recipe.

Remove the skin from the chicken thighs and toss in the flour.

Heat the oil in a wide skillet. Add the chicken and fry quickly until sealed and lightly browned, then remove from the skillet. Add the onion to the skillet and gently fry until soft. Add the garlic, bell peppers, tomatoes, and oregano, then bring to a boil, stirring constantly.

Arrange the chicken over the vegetables, season well with salt and pepper, then cover the skillet tightly and simmer for 20–25 minutes, or until the chicken is tender and the juices run clear when a skewer is inserted into the thickest part of the meat.

Taste and adjust the seasoning, if necessary, garnish with oregano, and serve with crusty whole-wheat bread.

chicken & herb fritters

makes 8

10 minutes

10 minutes

2¼ cups mashed potatoes, with
  butter added
9 oz/250 g cooked chicken, chopped
4½ oz/125 g cooked ham,
  finely chopped
1 tbsp dried mixed herbs
2 eggs, lightly beaten
salt and pepper

milk
2¼ cups fresh brown bread crumbs
corn oil, for pan-frying
fresh parsley sprigs, to garnish
mixed salad, to serve

*These fritters are delicious
served with a green salad, a
fresh vegetable salsa, or a
chili sauce dip.*

cook's tip

*A mixture of chopped
fresh tarragon and parsley
makes a flavorful addition
to these fritters.*

*To make a tomato sauce to
serve with the fritters, heat
¾ cup strained tomatoes and
4 tablespoons dry white wine.
Season, remove from the heat,
and add 4 tablespoons plain
yogurt. Return to the heat and
add chili powder to taste.*

Blend the mashed potatoes, chicken, ham, herbs, and 1 egg together in a
large bowl. Season well with salt and pepper.

Shape the mixture into flat patties or small balls.

Add a little milk to the second egg.

Place the bread crumbs on a plate. Dip the patties in the egg and milk
mixture, then roll in the bread crumbs to coat them completely.

Heat the oil in a large skillet and cook the fritters until they are golden
brown. Garnish with a fresh parsley sprig and serve with a mixed salad.

oaty chicken pieces

serves 4

15 minutes

40–50 minutes

¹/₃ cup porridge oats
1 tbsp chopped fresh rosemary
salt and pepper
4 skinless chicken quarters

1 egg white
²/₃ cup ricotta cheese
2 tsp whole-grain mustard
grated carrot salad, to serve

A lowfat chicken recipe with a refreshingly light, mustard-spiced sauce, which is ideal for a healthy lunch box or a light meal with salad.

variation

To make oaty chicken nuggets, chop up 4 skinless, boneless chicken breasts into small pieces. Reduce the cooking time by about 10 minutes and test for doneness. These nuggets would be ideal at a picnic, buffet, or children's party.

Preheat the oven to 400°F/200°C. Mix the oats, chopped rosemary, and salt and pepper to taste together in a large bowl.

Brush each piece of chicken evenly with egg white, then coat in the oat mixture. Place on a large cookie sheet and bake in the preheated oven for 40 minutes, or until the chicken is tender and the juices run clear when a skewer is inserted into the thickest part of the meat.

Mix the ricotta cheese and whole-grain mustard together in a bowl, then season to taste with salt and pepper. Serve with the chicken, hot or cold, and a grated carrot salad.

solomongundy

serves 4

10 minutes

1 large head lettuce, separated
  into leaves

4 chicken breasts, cooked and thinly
  sliced

8 rollmop herrings and their
  marinade

6 hard-cooked eggs, quartered

4^1/$_2$ oz/125 g cooked ham, sliced

4^1/$_2$ oz/125 g roast beef, sliced

4^1/$_2$ oz/125 g roast lamb, sliced

5^1/$_2$ oz/150 g snow peas, cooked

4^1/$_2$ oz/125 g seedless black grapes,

20 stuffed olives, sliced

12 shallots, boiled until tender

^{1}/$_2$ cup slivered almonds

^{1}/$_3$ cup golden raisins

2 oranges

salt and pepper

fresh mint sprig, to garnish

fresh crusty bread, to serve
  (optional)

*This recipe is ideally suited as
a cold platter for a buffet party
or a spectacular appetizer for
a special meal.*

variation

*Serve with cold, cooked
vegetables, such as sliced green
beans, baby corn, and cooked
beets, if you like.*

Spread out the lettuce leaves on a large oval platter.

Arrange the chicken in 3 sections on the platter.

Place the rollmop herrings, eggs, ham, beef, and lamb in lines or sections over the remainder of the platter.

Use the snow peas, grapes, olives, shallots, almonds, and golden raisins to fill in the spaces between the sections.

Grate the rind from the oranges and sprinkle over the whole platter. Peel and slice the oranges and add to the platter. Season well with salt and pepper. Garnish with the mint sprigs, sprinkle with the herring marinade, and serve with crusty bread, if you like.

chicken pan bagna

serves 6

10 minutes

–

1 large French baguette
1 garlic clove
½ cup olive oil
¾ oz/20 g canned anchovy fillets

2 oz/55 g cold roast chicken
2 large tomatoes, sliced
8 large, pitted black olives, chopped
pepper

Perfect for a picnic or packed lunch, this Mediterranean-style sandwich can be prepared in advance.

Using a sharp bread knife, cut the baguette in half lengthwise and open out.

Cut the garlic clove in half and rub over the bread.

Sprinkle the cut surface of the bread with the olive oil.

Drain the anchovies and reserve.

Thinly slice the chicken and arrange on top of the bread. Arrange the tomatoes and drained anchovies on top of the chicken.

Sprinkle over the chopped black olives and season with plenty of pepper. Sandwich the loaf back together and wrap tightly in foil until required. Cut into slices to serve.

cook's tip

Arrange a few fresh basil leaves in between the tomato slices to add a warm, spicy flavor. Use a good-quality olive oil in this recipe for extra flavor.

variation

You could use Italian ciabatta or olive-studded focaccia bread instead of the baguette, if you prefer. The last few years have seen an increasing interest in different breads and supermarkets now stock a wide range from home and abroad.

coronation chicken

serves 6

20 minutes

15 minutes

4 tbsp olive oil

2 lb/900 g chicken meat, diced

4¹/₂ oz/125 g rindless smoked
    bacon, diced

12 shallots

2 garlic cloves, crushed

1 tbsp mild curry powder

pepper

1¹/₄ cups mayonnaise

1 tbsp clear honey

1 tbsp chopped fresh parsley

3 oz/85 g seedless black grapes,
    quartered, to garnish

cold saffron rice, to serve

*This classic salad is good
as an appetizer or as part of
a buffet. Mango chutney
makes a tasty addition.*

Heat the oil in a large, heavy-bottomed skillet. Add the chicken, bacon,
shallots, garlic, and curry powder and cook gently for 15 minutes.

Spoon the mixture into a clean bowl.

Let the mixture cool completely, then season with pepper to taste.

Blend the mayonnaise with a little honey in a separate bowl, then add the
chopped parsley. Toss the chicken in the mixture.

Place the mixture in a deep serving dish, garnish with the grapes, and serve
with cold saffron rice.

cook's tip

*You can use this recipe to
fill a jacket potato or as a
sandwich filling, but cut the
chicken into smaller pieces.*

variation

*Add 2 tablespoons chopped fresh
apricots and 2 tablespoons slivered
almonds to the sauce with the
chopped parsley. For a healthier
version of this dish, replace the
mayonnaise with the same quantity
of plain yogurt and omit the honey,
otherwise the sauce will be too runny.*

potted
smoked chicken

serves 4–6

15 minutes, plus
4 hours chilling

–

12 oz/350 g chopped smoked chicken

pinch each of grated nutmeg
and mace

1 cup butter, softened, plus extra for
greasing

2 tbsp port

2 tbsp heavy cream

salt and pepper

fresh parsley sprig, to garnish

brown bread slices and fresh butter,
to serve

*This recipe can be made a
few days ahead and kept chilled
until needed. A food processor
makes light work of blending the
ingredients, but you can pound
by hand for a coarser mixture.*

cook's tip

*The Potted Smoked Chicken
can be kept in the refrigerator for
2–3 days, but no longer as it does
not contain any preservatives. It
may be stored in the freezer for
a maximum of 1 month.*

Place the smoked chicken, nutmeg, mace, a generous ½ cup of the butter,
port, and cream in a large bowl and season to taste with salt and pepper.

Pound until the mixture is very smooth or process in a food processor.

Transfer the mixture to individual earthenware pots or one large pot.

Cover each pot with greased parchment paper and weigh down with cans
or weights. Let chill in the refrigerator for 4 hours.

Heat the remaining butter in a small, heavy-bottomed pan until foaming.
Skim off the froth with a slotted spoon or pour the butter through a piece
of cheesecloth, to clarify.

Remove the parchment paper from the pots and pour a layer of clarified
butter on top of each. Chill until set.

Garnish with a parsley sprig and serve with brown bread and butter.

cheesy garlic drummers

serves 6

15 minutes

45–50 minutes

1 tbsp butter
1 garlic clove, crushed
3 tbsp chopped fresh parsley
generous ½ cup ricotta cheese
4 tbsp freshly grated
  Parmesan cheese

3 tbsp fresh bread crumbs
salt and pepper
12 chicken drumsticks
lemon slices, to garnish
mixed salad greens, to serve

Ideal for informal parties, these tasty chicken drumsticks can be prepared for cooking a day in advance. Instead of baking the chicken drumsticks, you could cook them on the barbecue instead.

cook's tip

Any strongly flavored cheese can be used instead of the Parmesan. Try a sharp Cheddar or use another Italian cheese, such as romano.

Freshly grated Parmesan has more "bite" than ready-packed grated Parmesan from supermarkets. Grate only as much as you need and wrap the rest up in foil—it will then keep for several months in the refrigerator.

Preheat the oven to 375°F/190°C. Melt the butter in a small pan. Add the garlic and fry gently, stirring constantly, for 1 minute without browning.

Remove the pan from the heat and stir in the parsley, cheeses, bread crumbs, and salt and pepper to taste.

Carefully loosen the skin around the chicken drumsticks.

Using a teaspoon, push about 1 tablespoon of the stuffing under the skin of each drumstick. Arrange the drumsticks in a large baking pan.

Bake in the preheated oven for 45 minutes, or until the chicken is tender and the juices run clear when a skewer is inserted into the thickest part of the meat. Serve hot or cold, garnished with lemon slices, with mixed salad greens.

chicken rarebit

serves 4

15 minutes

15–20 minutes

2¼ cups freshly grated
 Cheddar cheese
9 oz/250 g cooked chicken, shredded
1 tbsp butter
1 tbsp Worcestershire sauce
1 tsp English mustard powder

2 tsp all-purpose flour
4 tbsp mild beer
salt and pepper
4 slices bread
1 tbsp chopped fresh parsley,
 to garnish
cherry tomatoes, to serve

*A tasty dish that can be
served alone as a snack
or to accompany a light,
clear soup.*

Place the grated cheese, chicken, butter, Worcestershire sauce, mustard, flour, and beer in a small pan. Mix all the ingredients together, then season to taste with salt and pepper.

Gently bring the mixture to a boil, then remove the pan from the heat immediately.

Using a wooden spoon, beat until the mixture becomes creamy in texture. Let the mixture cool.

Preheat the broiler to high. Once the chicken mixture has cooled, toast the bread on both sides and spread with the chicken mixture.

Place under the hot broiler until bubbling and golden brown.

Sprinkle with a little chopped parsley and serve with cherry tomatoes.

waldorf summer
chicken salad

serves 4

10 minutes, plus
40 minutes standing

1 lb 2 oz/500 g red apples, diced
3 tbsp fresh lemon juice
2/3 cup lowfat mayonnaise
1 head celery
4 shallots, sliced
1 garlic clove, crushed

3/4 cup shelled walnuts, chopped
1 lb 2 oz/500 g cooked chicken, diced
1 romaine lettuce
pepper
sliced apple and walnuts, to garnish

This colorful and healthy dish is a variation of a classic salad. Served with crusty brown rolls, it is an ideal light meal for a summer's day.

cook's tip

Instead of the shallots, use scallions for a milder flavor. Trim the scallions and finely slice.

Soaking the apples in lemon juice prevents discoloration.

Place the apples in a nonmetallic bowl with the lemon juice and 1 tablespoon of the mayonnaise. Let stand for 40 minutes.

Separate the celery into stalks. Using a sharp knife, slice the celery stalks very thinly.

Add the celery, shallots, garlic, and walnuts to the apple mixture and mix together.

Stir in the remaining mayonnaise and blend thoroughly.

Add the cooked chicken to the bowl and mix well.

Line a glass salad bowl or serving dish with the lettuce leaves. Pile the chicken salad into the center, season well with pepper, and garnish with apple slices and walnuts.

old english
spicy chicken salad

 serves 4

 15 minutes

—

9 oz/250 g young spinach leaves
3 celery stalks
½ cucumber
2 scallions
3 tbsp chopped fresh parsley
12 oz/350 g boneless, roast chicken, thinly sliced
smoked almonds, to garnish (optional)

dressing

1-inch/2.5-cm piece fresh gingerroot, finely grated
3 tbsp olive oil
1 tbsp white wine vinegar
1 tbsp clear honey
½ tsp ground cinnamon
salt and pepper

For this simple, refreshing summer salad, you can use leftover roast chicken or ready-roasted chicken to save time. Add the dressing just before serving, or the spinach will lose its crispness.

variation

Fresh young spinach leaves go particularly well with fruits—try adding a few fresh raspberries or nectarine slices to make an even more refreshing salad.

Substitute corn salad for the spinach, if you prefer.

Thoroughly wash the spinach leaves under cold running water, then pat dry with paper towels.

Using a sharp knife, thinly slice the celery, cucumber, and scallions. Toss in a large bowl with the spinach leaves and parsley. Transfer to serving plates and arrange the chicken on top of the salad.

Mix all the dressing ingredients together in a screw-top jar and shake well. Season the dressing to taste with salt and pepper, then pour over the salad just before serving. Sprinkle with a few smoked almonds (if using).

suprême of chicken
with pear & blue cheese salad

serves 6

20 minutes

15–20 minutes

4 tbsp olive oil
6 shallots, sliced
1 garlic clove, crushed
2 tbsp chopped fresh tarragon
1 tbsp English mustard
salt and pepper
6 skinless, boneless chicken breasts
1 tbsp all-purpose flour
2/3 cup Chicken Stock
   (see page 5)
1 apple, finely diced

1 tbsp chopped walnuts
2 tbsp heavy cream

salad
9 oz/250 g cooked rice
2 large pears, diced
5 1/2 oz/150 g blue cheese, diced
1 red bell pepper, seeded and diced
1 tbsp chopped fresh cilantro
1 tbsp sesame oil

The sweetness of the pears complements perfectly the sharp taste of the blue cheese in this delicious warm salad.

Place the olive oil, shallots, garlic, tarragon, and mustard in a deep bowl. Season well with salt and pepper and mix the ingredients together thoroughly. Place the chicken in the marinade to coat completely, cover with plastic wrap, and let chill in the refrigerator for 4 hours.

Drain the chicken, reserving the marinade. Quickly fry the chicken in a large, deep nonstick skillet for 4 minutes on both sides, or until cooked through. Transfer the chicken to a warm serving dish.

Add the marinade to the skillet, bring to a boil, and sprinkle with the flour. Add the stock, apple, and walnuts and gently simmer for 5 minutes. Return the chicken to the sauce, add the cream, and cook for an additional 2 minutes.

Mix all the salad ingredients together, place a little on each plate, and top with a chicken breast and a spoonful of the sauce.

quick dishes

One of the marvelous qualities of chicken is that, when cut into small pieces, it can be cooked very quickly, which is welcome for those of us who are too busy to spend a lot of time preparing meals. In this section, you can select a tasty nutritious dish that won't take hours to make. Pasta makes a perfect partner for chicken as it is also quick to cook—Italian Chicken Spirals (see page 88) looks impressive and will fool guests into thinking that you have spent hours slaving away in the kitchen. Chicken breasts are cooked with a delicious basil, hazelnut, and garlic filling and then served on a bed of pasta, olives, and sun-dried tomatoes. Smaller cuts of chicken are also ideal for stir-fries that can be quickly cooked to produce tender, moist, and flavorful chicken. Speedy Peanut Pan-Fry (see page 80) is a crunchy stir-fry that is served with noodles. Risottos are also an excellent choice for when you are in a hurry—this chapter contains two risotto recipes, although the variations for risotto are endless!

harlequin chicken

serves 4

15 minutes

20–25 minutes

10 skinless, boneless chicken thighs
1 onion
1 each red, green, and yellow bell peppers
1 tbsp corn oil
14 oz/400 g canned chopped tomatoes

2 tbsp chopped fresh parsley
pepper

to serve

whole-wheat bread
green salad

This colorful, simple dish will tempt the appetites of all the family—it is ideal for toddlers, who enjoy the fun shapes of the multicolored bell peppers.

cook's tip

You can use dried parsley instead of fresh, but remember that you only need about half the quantity of dried to fresh.

If you are making this dish for small children, the chicken can be finely chopped or ground first.

Using a sharp knife, cut the chicken thighs into bite-size pieces.

Thinly slice the onion. Halve and seed the bell peppers and cut into small diamond shapes.

Heat the oil in a shallow skillet. Add the chicken and onion and fry quickly until golden.

Add the bell peppers, cook for 2–3 minutes, then stir in the chopped tomatoes and parsley and season to taste with pepper.

Cover tightly and simmer for 15 minutes, until the chicken and vegetables are tender. Serve hot with whole-wheat bread and a green salad.

steamed chicken &
spring vegetable pockets

serves 4

25 minutes

25–30 minutes

4 boneless, skinless chicken breasts
1 tsp ground lemon grass
salt and pepper
2 scallions, finely chopped
9 oz/250 g young carrots

9 oz/250 g young zucchini
2 celery stalks
1 tsp light soy sauce
9 oz/250 g spinach leaves
2 tsp sesame oil

A healthy recipe with a delicate Asian flavor, ideal for tender young summer vegetables. You'll need large spinach leaves to wrap around the chicken, but make sure they are not too tough.

Using a sharp knife, make a slit through one side of each chicken breast and enlarge each cut to form a pocket. Sprinkle the inside of the pocket with lemon grass and salt and pepper to taste. Tuck the scallions into the pockets.

Cut the carrots, zucchini, and celery into short thin sticks. Plunge into a pan of boiling water for 1 minute, then drain and toss in the soy sauce.

Pack the vegetables into the pockets in each chicken breast and fold over firmly to enclose. Reserve any remaining vegetables. Wash the spinach leaves thoroughly, then drain and pat dry with paper towels. Wrap the chicken breasts firmly in the spinach leaves to enclose completely. If the spinach leaves are too firm to wrap the chicken easily, steam them for a few seconds until they are softened and flexible.

Place the wrapped chicken in a steamer and steam over rapidly boiling water for 20–25 minutes, depending on size, until cooked through and tender.

Stir-fry any leftover vegetable sticks and spinach for 1–2 minutes in the sesame oil and serve with the chicken.

chicken with two
bell pepper sauce

serves 4

30 minutes

1 hour 20 minutes

2 tbsp olive oil

2 onions, finely chopped

2 garlic cloves, crushed

2 red bell peppers, seeded
   and chopped

good pinch of cayenne pepper

2 tsp tomato paste

2 yellow bell peppers, seeded and
   chopped

pinch of dried basil

salt and pepper

4 skinless, boneless chicken breasts

2/3 cup dry white wine

2/3 cup Chicken Stock
   (see page 5)

1 bouquet garni envelope

fresh herbs, to garnish

This quick and simple dish is colorful and healthy. It would be perfect for an impromptu lunch or supper dish.

cook's tip

Make your own bouquet garni by tying together sprigs of your favorite herbs with string, or wrap up dried herbs in a piece of cheesecloth. A popular combination is thyme, parsley, and bay.

Heat 1 tablespoon of the oil in each of 2 medium-size pans. Place half the chopped onions, 1 of the garlic cloves, the red bell peppers, the cayenne pepper, and the tomato paste in one pan. Place the remaining onion, garlic, yellow bell peppers, and basil in the other pan.

Cover each pan and cook over very low heat for 1 hour, or until the bell peppers are soft. If either mixture becomes dry, add a little water. Transfer each mixture separately to a food processor, and process until smooth. Strain both mixtures separately, then return the mixtures to the pans and season to taste with salt and pepper.

The sauces can be gently re-heated while the chicken is cooking.

Place the chicken breasts in a large skillet and add the wine and stock. Add the bouquet garni and bring the liquid to a simmer. Cook the chicken for 20 minutes, or until cooked through and tender.

To serve, pour a serving of each sauce on to 4 serving plates, slice the chicken breasts, and arrange on the plates. Garnish with fresh herbs and serve.

chicken risotto

à la milanese

serves 4

15 minutes

45–50 minutes

generous ½ cup butter

2 lb/900 g skinless, boneless chicken,
  thinly sliced

1 large onion, chopped

2⅓ cups risotto rice

2½ cups Chicken Stock
  (see page 5)

⅔ cup white wine

1 tsp crumbled saffron threads

salt and pepper

fresh flatleaf parsley sprigs,
  to garnish

½ cup freshly grated Parmesan
  cheese, to serve

*This famous dish is known
throughout the world, and it is
perhaps the best known of all
Italian risottos, although there
are many variations.*

Heat 4 tablespoons of the butter in a deep skillet. Add the chicken and
onion and fry until golden brown. Add the rice, stir well, and cook gently
for 5 minutes.

Heat the stock in a separate pan until boiling, then gradually add to the
rice a ladleful at a time. Reserve the last ladleful of stock. Add the white
wine, saffron, and salt and pepper to taste and mix well. Simmer gently for
20 minutes, stirring occasionally and adding more stock if the risotto
becomes too dry.

Remove the skillet from the heat and let stand for a few minutes. Just
before serving, add the reserved stock and simmer for an additional
10 minutes. Transfer the risotto to 4 large serving plates, garnish with the
parsley, and serve with the grated Parmesan cheese and remaining butter.

cook's tip

*A risotto should have moist but
separate grains. Stock should be
added a little at a time and only
when the previous addition has
been completely absorbed.*

variation

*The possibilities for risotto are endless—
try adding the following just at the end of
cooking time: cashew nuts and corn, lightly
sautéed zucchini and basil, or artichokes
and oyster mushrooms.*

elizabethan chicken

serves 4

20 minutes

45–50 minutes

1 tbsp butter

1 tbsp corn oil

4 skinless, boneless chicken breasts

4 shallots, finely chopped

2/3 cup Chicken Stock
(see page 5)

1 tbsp cider vinegar

6 oz/175 g halved seedless green grapes

1/2 cup heavy cream

1 tsp freshly grated nutmeg

salt and pepper

cornstarch, blended with a little stock
or water (optional)

selection of freshly cooked
vegetables, to serve

*Chicken is surprisingly delicious
when combined with fruits such
as grapes or gooseberries.*

variation

*If desired, add a little dry
white wine or vermouth with
the chicken stock and
cider vinegar.*

Heat the butter and oil in a wide skillet or flameproof casserole. Add the chicken breasts and quickly fry until golden brown, turning once. Remove the chicken breasts from the skillet and keep warm while you are cooking the shallots.

Add the chopped shallots to the skillet and fry gently until softened and lightly browned. Return the chicken breasts to the skillet.

Add the stock and cider vinegar, bring to a boil, then cover and simmer gently for 10–12 minutes, stirring occasionally, until the chicken is cooked through and tender.

Transfer the chicken to a large serving dish. Add the grapes, cream, and nutmeg to the skillet and heat through. Season to taste with salt and pepper. Add a little cornstarch paste and simmer for a few minutes to thicken the sauce, if you like. Pour the sauce over the chicken and serve with a selection of vegetables.

speedy peanut pan-fry

serves 4

20 minutes

10–15 minutes

10¹/₂ oz/300 g zucchini
9 oz/250 g baby corn
10¹/₂ oz/300 g white mushrooms
9 oz/250 g thread egg noodles
2 tbsp corn oil
1 tbsp sesame oil
8 boneless chicken thighs or
    4 breasts, thinly sliced

12 oz/350 g bean sprouts
4 tbsp smooth peanut butter
2 tbsp soy sauce
2 tbsp lime or lemon juice
pepper
¹/₃ cup roasted peanuts
fresh cilantro sprigs, to garnish

A complete entrée cooked within 10 minutes. Thread egg noodles are the ideal accompaniment because they can be cooked quickly and easily while the stir-fry sizzles.

cook's tip

Try serving this stir-fry with rice sticks. These are broad, pale, translucent ribbon noodles made from ground rice.

Using a sharp knife, thinly slice the zucchini, baby corn, and mushrooms.

Bring a large pan of lightly salted boiling water to a boil and cook the noodles for 3–4 minutes. Meanwhile, heat the corn oil and sesame oil in a large skillet or preheated wok. Add the chicken and fry over fairly high heat for 1 minute.

Add the sliced zucchini, baby corn, and mushrooms and stir-fry for 5 minutes.

Add the bean sprouts, peanut butter, soy sauce, lime or lemon juice, and pepper to taste, then cook for an additional 2 minutes.

Drain the noodles, transfer to a serving dish, and sprinkle with the peanuts. Serve with the stir-fried chicken and vegetables, garnished with fresh cilantro sprigs.

prosciutto-wrapped
chicken cushions

serves 4

30 minutes,
plus 1 hour chilling

35–40 minutes

4½ oz/125 g frozen spinach, thawed
generous ½ cup ricotta cheese
pinch of freshly grated nutmeg
salt and pepper
4 skinless, boneless chicken breasts,
   about 6 oz/175 g each
4 prosciutto slices
2 tbsp butter
1 tbsp olive oil

12 small onions or shallots
4½ oz/125 g white mushrooms,
   sliced
1 tbsp all-purpose flour
⅔ cup dry white or red wine
1¼ cups Chicken Stock
   (see page 5)
freshly cooked vegetables, to serve
   (optional)

*Chicken breasts are stuffed
with creamy ricotta, nutmeg,
and spinach, then wrapped with
wafer thin slices of prosciutto
and gently cooked in white wine.*

Place the spinach in a strainer and press out the water with a spoon, then place in a large bowl and stir in the ricotta and nutmeg. Season to taste with salt and pepper. Using a sharp knife, make a slit through one side of each chicken breast and enlarge each cut to form a pocket. Fill with the spinach mixture, reshape the chicken breasts, wrap each breast tightly in a slice of prosciutto, and secure with toothpicks. Cover and chill in the refrigerator.

Preheat the oven to 400°F/200°C. Heat the butter and oil in a large skillet. Add the chicken breasts and brown for 2 minutes on each side. Transfer the chicken to a large, shallow ovenproof dish and keep warm until required.

Add the onions and mushrooms to the skillet and fry for 2–3 minutes, or until lightly browned. Stir in the flour, then gradually add the wine and stock. Bring to a boil, stirring constantly. Season to taste with salt and pepper, then spoon the mixture around the chicken.

Cook the chicken, uncovered, in the preheated oven for 20 minutes. Turn the breasts over and cook for an additional 10 minutes, or until cooked through and tender. Remove the toothpicks and serve with the sauce and freshly cooked vegetables, if you like.

poached breast of chicken
with whiskey sauce

serves 6

20 minutes

35–40 minutes

2 tbsp butter
2 oz/55 g shredded leeks
2 oz/55 g diced carrot
2 oz/55 g diced celery
4 shallots, sliced
2½ cups Chicken Stock
  (see page 5)
6 skinless, boneless chicken breasts
4 tbsp whiskey
generous ¾ cup sour cream

2 tbsp freshly grated horseradish
1 tsp clear honey, warmed
1 tsp chopped fresh parsley
salt and pepper
fresh parsley sprigs, to garnish

to serve
mashed potatoes
butter or oil
freshly cooked vegetables

After cooking with stock and vegetables, chicken breasts are served with a velvety sauce made from whiskey and sour cream.

Melt the butter in a large, heavy-bottomed pan. Add the leeks, carrot, celery, and shallots and cook for 3 minutes. Add half the stock and cook for 8 minutes.

Add the remaining stock and bring to a boil, then add the chicken breasts and cook for 10 minutes, or until cooked through and tender.

Remove the chicken from the pan and thinly slice. Place on a large, hot serving dish and keep warm until required.

Heat the whiskey in another pan until reduced by half. Strain the stock through a fine strainer, then add to the pan and simmer until it is reduced by half.

Add the sour cream, horseradish, and honey and heat gently. Add the parsley and season to taste with salt and pepper. Stir until well blended.

Make vegetable patties by mixing the leftover vegetables with mashed potatoes and shaping into round cakes. Fry in a little butter or oil until golden brown.

Pour a little of the whiskey sauce around the chicken and pour the remaining sauce into a sauceboat. Garnish with the parsley sprig and serve with the vegetable patties and vegetables.

devilled chicken

serves 4

20 minutes

45 minutes

3 tbsp all-purpose flour
1 tsp cayenne pepper
1 tsp paprika
12 oz/350 g skinless, boneless
    chicken breast, diced
2 tbsp butter
1 onion, finely chopped

2 cups milk, warmed
4 tbsp apple purée
4½ oz/125 g seedless green grapes
⅔ cup sour cream
paprika, for sprinkling

Chicken is spiked with cayenne pepper and paprika and finished off with a fruity sauce.

Place the flour, cayenne pepper, and paprika in a large, shallow dish and mix together. Add the diced chicken and turn to coat. Shake off any excess flour.

Melt the butter in a large, heavy-bottomed pan. Add the chicken and onion and gently fry for 4 minutes.

Stir in the flour and spice mixture. Add the milk slowly, stirring constantly, until the sauce thickens.

Simmer until the sauce is smooth, then add the apple purée and grapes and simmer gently for 20 minutes.

Transfer the chicken and devilled sauce to a large, warm serving dish, or individual plates, and top with sour cream and a sprinkle of paprika.

cook's tip

Add more paprika if desired—as it is quite a mild spice, you can add plenty without it being too overpowering.

variation

For a healthier alternative to sour cream, use plain yogurt.

italian chicken spirals

serves 4

15 minutes

20 minutes

4 skinless, boneless chicken breasts
1 oz/25 g fresh basil leaves
2 tbsp hazelnuts
1 garlic clove, crushed
salt and pepper
9 oz/250 g dried whole-wheat
    pasta spirals

2 sun-dried tomatoes
1 tbsp lemon juice
1 tbsp olive oil
1 tbsp capers
1/3 cup black olives

Steaming allows you to cook without fat, and these little foil pockets retain all the natural juices of the chicken while cooking conveniently over the pasta as it boils.

variation

Sun-dried tomatoes have a wonderful, rich flavor, but if you can't find them, use fresh tomatoes.

Beat the chicken breasts with a rolling pin to flatten evenly.

Place the basil and hazelnuts in a food processor and process until finely chopped. Transfer to a bowl and stir in the garlic and salt and pepper to taste. Spread the basil mixture over the chicken breasts and roll up from one short end to enclose the filling. Wrap the chicken rolls tightly in foil so that they hold their shape, then seal the ends well.

Bring a large pan of lightly salted water to a boil. Add the pasta, return to a boil, and cook until tender but still firm to the bite.

Place the chicken pockets in a steamer basket or colander set over the pan, cover tightly, and steam for 10 minutes. Meanwhile, dice the tomatoes.

Drain the pasta and return to the pan. Add the lemon juice, olive oil, diced tomatoes, capers, and olives and heat through until piping hot.

Insert a skewer into the chicken to make sure that the juices run clear and not pink, then slice the chicken, arrange over the pasta, and serve.

garlicky chicken cushions

serves 4

20 minutes

50 minutes

4 part-boned chicken breasts
4¹⁄₂ oz/125 g frozen spinach, thawed
²⁄₃ cup ricotta cheese
2 garlic cloves, crushed
salt and pepper
1 tbsp olive oil
1 onion, chopped

1 red bell pepper, seeded and sliced
14 oz/400 g canned chopped
   tomatoes
6 tbsp wine or Chicken Stock
   (see page 5)
10 stuffed olives, sliced
freshly cooked pasta, to serve

Stuffed with creamy ricotta, spinach, and garlic, then gently cooked in a rich tomato sauce, this is a suitable dish to make ahead of time.

Preheat the oven to 400°F/200°C. Make a slit between the skin and meat on one side of each chicken breast. Lift the skin to form a pocket, being careful to leave the skin attached to the other side.

Place the spinach in a strainer and press out the water with a spoon. Transfer to a bowl and stir in the ricotta and half the garlic. Season to taste with salt and pepper.

Spoon the spinach mixture under the skin of each chicken breast, then secure the edge of the skin with toothpicks.

Heat the oil in a skillet, add the onion, and fry for 1 minute, stirring. Add the remaining garlic and red bell pepper and cook for 2 minutes. Stir in the tomatoes, wine, olives, and seasoning. If preparing in advance, remove the skillet from the heat and set aside. Let the chicken chill in the refrigerator.

Bring the sauce to a boil, pour into a large casserole, and arrange the chicken breasts on top in a single layer.

Cook, uncovered, in the preheated oven for 35 minutes, or until the chicken is golden and tender and the juices run clear when a skewer is inserted into the thickest part of the meat. Spoon a little of the sauce over the chicken breasts, then transfer to serving plates and serve with freshly cooked pasta.

chicken strips & dips

serves 2

10 minutes

10–15 minutes

2 boneless chicken breasts
2 tbsp all-purpose flour
1 tbsp corn oil

peanut dip

3 tbsp smooth or crunchy peanut
    butter
4 tbsp plain yogurt
1 tsp grated orange rind
orange juice (optional)

tomato dip

1 tomato
5 tbsp mascarpone cheese
2 tsp tomato paste
1 tsp snipped fresh chives

selection of vegetables, cut into
    sticks, to serve

*Very simple to make and easy to
eat with fingers, this dish can be
served warm for a light lunch or
cold as part of a buffet.*

variation

*For a lower-fat alternative,
poach the strips of chicken in a
small amount of boiling chicken
stock for 6–8 minutes.*

*For a refreshing guacamole dip,
combine 1 mashed avocado,
2 finely chopped scallions,
1 chopped tomato, 1 crushed garlic
clove, and a squeeze of lemon juice.
Remember to add the lemon
juice immediately after the
avocado has been mashed
to prevent discoloration.*

Using a sharp knife, slice the chicken into fairly thin strips and toss in the
flour to coat.

Heat the oil in a large, nonstick skillet. Add the chicken and fry until golden
and thoroughly cooked. Remove the chicken strips from the skillet and
drain well on paper towels.

To make the Peanut Dip, mix all the ingredients together in a bowl (if liked,
add a little orange juice to thin the consistency).

To make the Tomato Dip, chop the tomato and place in a small bowl. Add
the remaining ingredients and mix together.

Serve the chicken strips with the dips and a selection of vegetable sticks
for dipping.

chicken lady jayne

serves 4

15 minutes

15 minutes

4 chicken suprêmes or breasts, about
   4¹/₂ oz/125 g each

4 tbsp corn oil

8 shallots, sliced

grated rind and juice of 1 lemon

2 tsp Worcestershire sauce

4 tbsp Chicken Stock
   (see page 5)

1 tbsp chopped fresh parsley

3 tbsp coffee-flavored liqueur

3 tbsp brandy, warmed

If you prefer, just use boneless chicken breasts in this recipe. This dish has a surprising combination of coffee and brandy flavors.

cook's tip

Flattening the suprêmes or chicken breasts means that they take less time to cook.

Place the chicken suprêmes or breasts on a cutting board, cover with plastic wrap, and pound them until flattened with a wooden meat mallet or a rolling pin.

Heat the oil in a large skillet. Add the chicken and fry for 3 minutes on each side. Add the shallots and cook for an additional 3 minutes.

Sprinkle with lemon rind and juice and add the Worcestershire sauce and stock. Cook for 2 minutes, then sprinkle with the chopped parsley.

Add the coffee-flavored liqueur and brandy, then ignite with a taper or long match. Cook until the flames die down and serve.

golden glazed chicken

serves 6

15 minutes, plus
1 hour marinating

30 minutes

6 boneless chicken breasts
1 tsp ground turmeric
1 tbsp whole-grain mustard
1¼ cups orange juice
2 tbsp clear honey
2 tbsp corn oil

1¾ cups long-grain rice
salt
1 orange
3 tbsp chopped fresh mint
fresh mint sprigs, to garnish

A glossy glaze with sweet and fruity flavors coats chicken breasts in this tasty recipe.

Using a sharp knife, mark the surface of the chicken breasts in a diamond pattern and place in a large bowl. Mix the turmeric, mustard, orange juice, and honey together in a small bowl and pour over the chicken. Let chill in the refrigerator for 1 hour.

Lift the chicken from the marinade and pat dry on paper towels.

Heat the oil in a wide skillet. Add the chicken and sauté until golden, turning once. Drain off any excess oil. Pour over the marinade, cover, and simmer for 10–15 minutes, or until the chicken is cooked through and tender.

Boil the rice in lightly salted water until tender and drain well. Finely grate the rind from the orange and stir into the rice with the mint.

variation

To make a slightly sharper sauce, use a small grapefruit instead of the orange.

Using a sharp knife, remove the peel and white pith from the orange and cut the flesh into segments.

Serve the chicken with the orange and mint rice, garnished with orange segments and mint sprigs.

mediterranean
chicken pockets

serves 6

20 minutes

20 minutes

1 tbsp olive oil
6 skinless chicken breast fillets
9 oz/250 g mozzarella cheese
1 lb 2 oz/500 g zucchini, sliced
6 large tomatoes, sliced

pepper
1 small bunch of fresh basil
   or oregano
freshly cooked pasta,
   to serve

This method of cooking makes the chicken aromatic and succulent. It also reduces the amount of oil needed since the chicken and vegetables cook in their own juices.

cook's tip

To aid cooking, place the vegetables and chicken on the shiny side of the foil so that once the pocket is wrapped up the dull surface of the foil is facing outward. This ensures that the heat is absorbed into the pocket and not reflected away from it.

Preheat the oven to 400°F/200°C. Cut 6 pieces of foil each about 10 inches/25 cm square. Brush the foil squares lightly with oil and reserve until required.

Using a sharp knife, slash each chicken breast at intervals, then slice the mozzarella cheese and place between the cuts in the chicken.

Divide the zucchini and tomatoes between the pieces of foil. Sprinkle with pepper to taste. Tear or coarsely chop the basil or oregano and scatter over the vegetables in each pocket.

Place a chicken breast on top of each pile of vegetables, then wrap in the foil to enclose the chicken and vegetables, tucking in the ends.

Place on a cookie sheet and bake in the preheated oven for 30 minutes, or until the chicken is tender and the juices run clear when a skewer is inserted into the thickest part of the meat.

To serve, unwrap each foil pocket and serve with pasta.

chicken, corn
& snow pea sauté

serves 4

15 minutes

10 minutes

4 skinless, boneless chicken breasts
9 oz/250 g baby corn
9 oz/250 g snow peas
2 tbsp corn oil
1 tbsp sherry vinegar

1 tbsp clear honey
1 tbsp light soy sauce
1 tbsp sunflower seeds
pepper
freshly cooked egg noodles, to serve

This quick and healthy dish is stir-fried, which means you need use only the minimum of fat. If you don't have a wok, use a wide skillet instead.

cook's tip

Rice vinegar or balsamic vinegar would make a good substitute for the sherry vinegar.

Using a sharp knife, slice the chicken breasts into long, thin strips. Cut the baby corn in half lengthwise and trim the snow peas. Reserve the vegetables until required.

Heat the oil in a preheated wok or a wide skillet. Add the chicken and fry over fairly high heat, stirring constantly, for 1 minute.

Add the baby corn and snow peas and stir-fry over medium heat for 5–8 minutes, or until evenly cooked.

Mix the sherry vinegar, honey, and soy sauce together and stir into the pan with the sunflower seeds. Season to taste with pepper. Cook, stirring constantly, for 1 minute. Serve hot with freshly cooked egg noodles.

savory chicken
sausages

 serves 4–6

 10 minutes

 6–10 minutes

3 cups fresh bread crumbs
9 oz/250 g cooked chicken, ground
1 small leek, finely chopped
pinch each of mixed herbs and
   mustard powder
salt and pepper

2 eggs, separated
4 tbsp milk
crisp bread crumbs, for coating
2 tbsp beef drippings
fresh parsley sprigs, to garnish

Served with a smooth creamy tomato sauce, this makes an excellent light lunch with freshly baked cheese bread.

Mix the bread crumbs, ground chicken, leek, mixed herbs, and mustard powder together in a large bowl, and season to taste with salt and pepper.

Add 1 whole egg and an egg yolk with a little milk to bind the mixture.

Divide the mixture into 6 or 8 portions and, using your hands, shape into thick or thin sausages.

Whisk the remaining egg white in a large, clean bowl until frothy. Coat the sausages first in the egg white and then in the crisp bread crumbs. Heat the drippings in a skillet. Add the the sausages and fry for 6 minutes, or until golden brown. Transfer to individual plates, garnish with parsley sprigs, and serve.

variation

If you want to lower the saturated fat content of this recipe, use a little oil for frying instead of the drippings.

golden chicken risotto

 serves 4

 10 minutes

 25 minutes

2 tbsp corn oil
1 tbsp butter
1 leek, thinly sliced
1 large yellow bell pepper, seeded
  and diced
3 skinless, boneless chicken
  breasts, diced
scant 1²/3 cups risotto rice
few saffron threads

salt and pepper
6¼ cups Chicken Stock
  (see page 5)
7 oz/200 g canned corn
¹/3 cup toasted unsalted peanuts
¹/2 cup freshly grated Parmesan
  cheese

If you prefer, ordinary long-grain rice can be used instead of risotto rice, but it won't give you the traditional, deliciously creamy texture that is typical of Italian risottos.

cook's tip

Risottos can be frozen, before adding the Parmesan cheese, for up to 1 month, but remember to re-heat this risotto thoroughly as it contains chicken.

Heat the oil and butter in a large, heavy-bottomed pan. Add the leek and bell pepper and fry for 1 minute, then stir in the chicken and cook, stirring constantly, until golden brown.

Stir in the rice and cook for 2–3 minutes.

Stir in the saffron threads and add salt and pepper to taste. Add the stock, a ladleful at a time, then cover and cook over low heat, stirring occasionally, for 20 minutes, until the rice is tender and most of the liquid is absorbed. Do not let the risotto dry out—add more stock if necessary.

Stir in the corn, peanuts, and Parmesan cheese, then taste and adjust the seasoning if necessary. Serve hot.

quick chicken bake

serves 4

15 minutes, plus
40 minutes cooking

40–45 minutes

1 lb 2 oz/500 g ground chicken
1 large onion, finely chopped
2 carrots, finely diced
3 tbsp all-purpose flour
1 tbsp tomato paste
1¼ cups Chicken Stock
(see page 5)
salt and pepper

pinch of fresh thyme
2 lb/900 g boiled potatoes, creamed
with butter and milk and highly
seasoned
¾ cup freshly grated Cheddar
cheese
freshly cooked peas, to serve

*This recipe is a type of cottage
pie—a traditional English dish.
Add vegetables and herbs of your
choice, depending on what you
have at hand.*

variation

*Instead of Cheddar cheese,
sprinkle grated Monterey Jack
cheese over the top. Alternatively,
you could use a mixture of cheeses.*

Dry-fry the chicken, onion, and carrots in a nonstick skillet for
5 minutes, stirring frequently.

Sprinkle the chicken mixture with the flour and simmer for an additional
2 minutes.

Gradually blend in the tomato paste and stock, then simmer for
15 minutes. Season to taste with salt and pepper and add the thyme.

Transfer the chicken and vegetable mixture to an ovenproof casserole and
let cool.

Preheat the oven to 400°F/200°C. Spoon the mashed potatoes over the
chicken mixture and sprinkle with the cheese. Bake in the preheated oven
for 20 minutes, or until the cheese is bubbling and golden, then serve with
freshly cooked peas.

tom's toad in the hole

serves 4–6

15 minutes, plus
1 hour 35 minutes standing

40–45 minutes

²/₃ cup all-purpose flour
pinch of salt
1 egg, beaten
generous ³/₄ cup milk
¹/₃ cup water

2 tbsp beef drippings
9 oz/250 g skinless, boneless
   chicken breasts
9 oz/250 g sausages

*This unusual recipe uses
chicken and sausages, which is
then made into individual
bite-size pieces.*

Mix the flour and salt in a bowl, then make a well in the center and add the beaten egg.

Add half the milk and, using a wooden spoon, work in the flour slowly.

Beat the mixture until smooth, then add the remaining milk and water.

Beat again until the mixture is smooth. Let the mixture stand for at least 1 hour.

Preheat the oven to 425°F/220°C. Add the drippings to individual baking pans or to 1 large baking pan. Cut up the chicken and sausages so that you get a generous piece in each individual pan or several scattered around the large pan.

variation

*Use skinless, boneless chicken legs
instead of chicken breasts in the
recipe. Cut up as directed.*

Heat in the preheated oven for 5 minutes, or until very hot. Remove the pans from the oven and pour in the batter, leaving space for the mixture to expand.

Return to the oven to cook for 35 minutes, or until risen and golden brown. Do not open the oven door for at least 30 minutes. Serve hot.

casseroles
& roasts

Long, slow cooking means meltingly succulent meat with a good, rich flavor.

Because chicken itself does not have a strong flavor, it marries happily with

almost any other ingredient, herb, or spice. The recipes in this section are

drawn from many cuisines from around the world, and there are dishes

from Italy, France, Hungary, the Caribbean, and the UK. French classics

include Bourguignonne of Chicken (see page 120) and Brittany Chicken

Casserole (see page 136).

The aroma of roasting chicken is always tempting and this section

includes the traditional roast chicken as well as many other imaginative

treatments. Unusual stuffings to try are zucchini and lime, marmalade,

or oat and herb stuffing. Many of the recipes in this section exploit the

complementary flavors of chicken and fruits and there are some enticing

taste combinations including cranberries, black cherries, apples, peaches,

oranges, and mangoes.

rustic chicken

& orange pot

serves 4

20 minutes

1 hour 10 minutes

8 chicken drumsticks, skinned
1 tbsp whole-wheat flour
1 tbsp olive oil
2 red onions
1 garlic clove, crushed
1 tsp fennel seeds
1 bay leaf
finely grated rind and juice of
 1 small orange

14 oz/400 g canned chopped
 tomatoes
14 oz/400 g canned cannellini or
 flageolet beans, drained and rinsed
salt and pepper

topping
3 thick slices whole-wheat bread
2 tsp olive oil

Low in fat and high in fiber, this colorful casserole makes a healthy and hearty meal.

cook's tip

Choose beans that are canned in water with no added sugar or salt. Drain and rinse well before use.

Preheat the oven to 375°F/190°C. Toss the chicken drumsticks in the flour to coat evenly. Heat the oil in a nonstick or heavy-bottomed pan. Add the chicken and fry over fairly high heat, turning frequently, until golden brown. Transfer to a large, ovenproof casserole and keep warm until required.

Slice the red onions into thin wedges. Add to the pan and cook for a few minutes, until lightly browned. Stir in the garlic.

Add the fennel seeds, bay leaf, orange rind and juice, tomatoes, and beans and season to taste with salt and pepper.

Cover tightly and cook in the preheated oven for 30–35 minutes, or until the chicken is tender and the juices run clear when a skewer is inserted into the thickest part of the meat.

Cut the bread into small dice and toss in the oil. Remove the lid from the casserole and top with the bread cubes. Bake for an additional 15–20 minutes, or until the bread is golden and crisp. Serve hot.

spiced chicken casserole

serves 4–6

15 minutes

2 hours 10 minutes

3 tbsp olive oil

2 lb/900 g chicken, sliced

10 shallots

3 carrots, chopped

1/2 cup peeled and skinned chestnuts, sliced

1/2 cup slivered almonds, toasted

1 tsp freshly grated nutmeg

3 tsp ground cinnamon

1 1/4 cups white wine

1 1/4 cups Chicken Stock (see page 5)

3/4 cup white wine vinegar

1 tbsp chopped fresh tarragon

1 tbsp chopped fresh parsley

1 tbsp chopped fresh thyme

grated rind of 1 orange

1 tbsp raw brown sugar

salt and pepper

4 1/2 oz/125 g seedless black grapes, halved

fresh herbs, to garnish

freshly cooked wild rice, to serve

Spices, herbs, fruits, nuts, and vegetables are combined to make an appealing casserole with lots of flavor.

Heat the oil in a large, heavy-bottomed pan. Add the chicken, shallots, and carrots and fry for 6 minutes, or until browned.

Add the remaining ingredients, except the grapes, and simmer over low heat for 2 hours, or until the meat is very tender. Stir occasionally.

Add the grapes just before serving. Transfer to individual plates, garnish with fresh herbs, and serve with freshly cooked wild rice.

cook's tip

This casserole would also be delicious served with thick slices of crusty whole-wheat bread to soak up the sauce.

variation

Experiment with different types of nuts and fruits—try sunflower seeds instead of the almonds, and add 2 fresh apricots, chopped.

country chicken hotchpotch

serves 4

20 minutes

2 hours

4 chicken quarters
6 potatoes
salt and pepper
2 fresh thyme sprigs
2 fresh rosemary sprigs
2 bay leaves

7 oz/200 g rindless smoked lean
  bacon, diced
1 large onion, finely chopped
7 oz/200 g sliced carrots
2/3 cup stout
2 tbsp melted butter

*There are many regional versions
of hotchpotch, all using fresh, local
ingredients. Now there are an
endless variety of ingredients
available all year, perfect for
traditional one-pot cooking.*

Preheat the oven to 300°F/150°C. Remove the skin from the chicken
quarters, if you like. Cut the potatoes into 1/4-inch/5-mm slices.

Arrange a layer of potato slices in the bottom of a wide casserole. Season
to taste with salt and pepper, then add the thyme, rosemary, and
bay leaves.

Top with the chicken quarters, then sprinkle with the bacon, onion, and
carrots. Season well with salt and pepper. Arrange the remaining potato
slices on top, overlapping slightly.

Pour over the stout, brush the potatoes with the melted butter, and cover
with a lid.

Bake in the preheated oven for 2 hours, uncovering for the last 30 minutes
to allow the potatoes to brown. Serve hot.

cook's tip

*Serve the hotchpotch
with Dumplings
(see page 127) for a
truly hearty meal.*

variation

*This dish is also delicious with
stewing lamb, cut into chunks.
You can add different vegetables
depending on what is in season—
try leeks and rutabaga for a slightly
sweeter flavor.*

fricassee of chicken in lime sauce

serves 4

30 minutes

1 hour 45 minutes

1 large chicken, cut into small
  portions
scant ½ cup all-purpose flour,
  seasoned
2 tbsp corn oil
1 lb 2 oz/500 g pearl onions or
  shallots, sliced
1 each green and red bell pepper,
  seeded and thinly sliced

⅔ cup Chicken Stock
  (see page 5)
grated rind and juice of 2 limes
2 fresh chiles, chopped
2 tbsp oyster sauce
1 tsp Worcestershire sauce
salt and pepper

The addition of lime juice and lime rind adds a delicious tangy flavor to this chicken casserole.

Preheat the oven to 375°F/190°C. Coat the chicken pieces in the seasoned flour. Heat the oil in a large skillet. Add the chicken and cook for 4 minutes, or until browned all over.

Using a slotted spoon, transfer the chicken to a large, deep casserole and sprinkle with the sliced onions. Keep warm until required.

Slowly fry the bell peppers in the juices remaining in the skillet. Add the stock, lime rind, and juice and cook for an additional 5 minutes.

cook's tip

Try this casserole with a cheese biscuit topping. About 30 minutes before the end of cooking time, simply top with rounds cut from cheese biscuit dough.

Add the chiles, oyster sauce, and Worcestershire sauce. Season to taste with salt and pepper.

Pour the bell peppers and juices over the chicken and onions.

Cover the casserole with a lid or foil.

Cook in the center of the preheated oven for 1½ hours, or until the chicken is very tender, then serve.

bourguignonne of chicken

serves 4–6

20 minutes

1 hour 40 minutes

4 tbsp corn oil

2 lb/900 g skinless chicken, diced

9 oz/250 g white mushrooms

4½ oz/125 g rindless smoked bacon, diced

16 shallots

2 garlic cloves, crushed

1 tbsp all-purpose flour

⅔ cup white Burgundy wine

⅔ cup Chicken Stock (see page 5)

1 bouquet garni (1 bay leaf, 1 fresh thyme sprig, 1 celery stalk, 1 fresh parsley sprig, and 1 fresh sage sprig tied together with string)

salt and pepper

to serve

Croutons (see page 25)

selection of cooked vegetables

A recipe based on a classic French dish. Use a good-quality wine when making this casserole.

cook's tip

A good-quality red wine can be used instead of the white wine, to produce a rich, glossy red sauce.

Preheat the oven to 300°F/150°C. Heat the oil in a flameproof casserole. Add the chicken and cook until browned all over. Remove from the casserole with a slotted spoon and reserve.

Add the mushrooms, bacon, shallots, and garlic to the casserole and cook for 4 minutes.

Return the chicken to the casserole and sprinkle with flour. Cook for an additional 2 minutes, stirring. Add the wine and stock and stir until boiling. Add the bouquet garni and season well with salt and pepper.

Cover the casserole and bake in the center of the preheated oven for 1½ hours. Remove and discard the bouquet garni.

Fry some heart-shaped Croutons (about 8 large ones) and serve with the Bourguignonne and a selection of vegetables.

country chicken bake

serves 4

20 minutes

35 minutes

2 tbsp corn oil

4 chicken quarters

16 small whole onions

3 celery stalks, sliced

14 oz/400 g canned red kidney beans, drained and rinsed

4 tomatoes, quartered

generous ³/4 cup dry hard cider or Chicken Stock (see page 5)

4 tbsp chopped fresh parsley

salt and pepper

1 tsp paprika

4 tbsp butter

12 slices French bread

This economical bake is a complete meal—its crusty, herb-flavored French bread topping mops up the tasty juices, and means there's no need to serve potatoes or rice separately.

Preheat the oven to 400°F/200°C. Heat the oil in a large, flameproof casserole. Add the chicken quarters, 2 at a time, and fry until golden. Using a slotted spoon, remove the chicken from the casserole and reserve until required.

Add the onions and fry, turning occasionally, until golden brown. Add the celery and cook for 2–3 minutes. Return the chicken to the casserole, then stir in the beans, tomatoes, hard cider, and half the parsley. Season to taste with salt and pepper and sprinkle with the paprika.

Cover and cook in the preheated oven for 20–25 minutes, or until the chicken is tender and the juices run clear when a skewer is inserted into the thickest part of the meat.

Mix the remaining parsley and butter together, then spread evenly over the French bread. Uncover the casserole, arrange the bread slices overlapping on top, and bake for an additional 10–12 minutes, or until golden and crisp.

cook's tip

Add a crushed garlic clove to the parsley butter for extra flavor.

variation

For a more Italian-tasting dish, replace the garlic and parsley bread topping with Pesto Toasts (see page 208).

hungarian chicken goulash

serves 6

20 minutes

1 hour 40 minutes

2 lb/900 g chicken, diced
scant 1/2 cup all-purpose flour,
    seasoned with 1 tsp paprika, salt,
    and pepper
2 tbsp olive oil
2 tbsp butter
1 onion, sliced
24 shallots
1 each red and green bell pepper,
    seeded and chopped
1 tbsp paprika
1 tsp fresh rosemary, crushed

4 tbsp tomato paste
1 1/4 cups Chicken Stock (see page 5)
2/3 cup claret
14 oz/400 g canned chopped
    tomatoes

to garnish
sour cream
1 tbsp chopped fresh parsley

to serve
chunks of bread
crisp salad

Goulash is traditionally made with beef, but this recipe successfully uses chicken instead. To reduce the fat, use a lowfat cream instead of the sour cream.

variation

Serve the goulash with buttered ribbon noodles instead of bread. For an authentic touch, try a Hungarian red wine instead of the claret.

Preheat the oven to 325°F/160°C. Toss the chicken in the seasoned flour until it is coated all over.

Heat the oil and butter in a flameproof casserole. Add the onion, shallots, and bell peppers and fry for 3 minutes.

Add the chicken and cook for an additional 4 minutes.

Sprinkle with the paprika and rosemary.

Add the tomato paste, stock, claret, and chopped tomatoes, cover, and cook in the center of the preheated oven for 1 1/2 hours, or until the chicken is very tender.

Remove the casserole from the oven, let stand for 4 minutes, then garnish with the sour cream and parsley.

Serve with chunks of bread and a crisp salad.

country chicken braise
with rosemary dumplings

serves 4

30 minutes

1 hour 20 minutes

4 chicken quarters
2 tbsp corn oil
2 leeks
9 oz/250 g carrots, chopped
9 oz/250 g parsnips, chopped
2 small turnips, chopped
2½ cups Chicken Stock
   (see page 5)
3 tbsp Worcestershire sauce

2 fresh rosemary sprigs
salt and pepper

dumplings
scant 1½ cups self-rising flour
scant 1 cup shredded suet
1 tbsp chopped fresh rosemary
   leaves
salt and pepper
about 2–3 tbsp cold water

Root vegetables are always cheap and nutritious, and combined with chicken they make tasty and economical casseroles.

Remove the skin from the chicken, if you prefer. Heat the oil in a large, flameproof casserole or heavy-bottomed pan. Add the chicken and fry until golden. Using a slotted spoon, remove the chicken from the casserole. Drain off the excess fat.

Slice the leeks and add to the casserole together with the carrots, parsnips, and turnips. Cook for 5 minutes, or until the vegetables are lightly colored. Return the chicken to the casserole.

Add the stock, Worcestershire sauce, and rosemary and season to taste with salt and pepper, then bring to a boil.

Reduce the heat, cover, and simmer gently for 50 minutes, or until the chicken is tender and the juices run clear when a skewer is inserted into the thickest part of the meat.

To make the dumplings, mix the flour, suet, rosemary, and salt and pepper together in a large bowl. Stir in just enough water to form a firm dough.

Form into 8 small balls between the palms of your hands and place on top of the chicken and vegetables. Cover and simmer for an additional 10–12 minutes, or until the dumplings are well risen. Serve immediately with the casserole.

chicken with shallots in
exotic mushroom & ginger sauce

serves 6–8

30 minutes

1 hour 50 minutes

2 lb/900 g skinless chicken, diced
scant ½ cup all-purpose flour, seasoned
6 tbsp sesame oil
32 shallots, sliced
1 lb 2 oz/500 g exotic mushrooms, coarsely chopped
1¼ cups Chicken Stock (see page 5)

2 tbsp Worcestershire sauce
1 tbsp clear honey
2 tbsp grated fresh gingerroot
salt and pepper
⅔ cup plain yogurt
fresh flatleaf parsley sprigs, to garnish
wild rice and white rice, to serve

This recipe has an Asian flavor, which can be further enhanced with chopped scallions, cinnamon, and lemon grass.

cook's tip

Mushrooms can be stored in the refrigerator for 24–36 hours. Keep them in paper bags as they "sweat" in plastic. Exotic mushrooms must be washed thoroughly.

Preheat the oven to 300°F/150°C. Toss the chicken in the seasoned flour. Heat the oil in a large skillet. Add the chicken and cook for 4 minutes, or until browned all over. Transfer to a large, deep casserole and keep warm until required.

Gently fry the shallots and mushrooms in the juices remaining in the skillet. Add the stock, Worcestershire sauce, honey, and gingerroot, then season to taste with salt and pepper.

Pour the mixture over the chicken, cover, and cook in the center of the preheated oven for 1½ hours, or until the chicken is very tender.

Add the yogurt and cook for an additional 10 minutes. Transfer the casserole to individual plates, garnish with parsley sprigs, and serve with a mixture of wild rice and white rice.

jamaican hotchpotch

serves 4

30 minutes

1 hour 20 minutes

2 tsp corn oil

4 chicken drumsticks

4 chicken thighs

1 onion

1 lb 10 oz/750 g piece pumpkin
  or squash

1 green bell pepper

1-inch/2.5-cm piece fresh gingerroot,
  finely chopped

14 oz/400 g canned chopped
  tomatoes

1 1/4 cups Chicken Stock
  (see page 5)

scant 1/3 cup split red lentils

garlic salt and cayenne pepper

12 oz/350 g canned corn

crusty bread, to serve

A tasty way to make chicken pieces go a long way, this hearty casserole, spiced with the warm, subtle flavor of ginger, is a good choice for a Halloween party.

variation

If you can't find fresh gingerroot, add 1 teaspoon ground allspice for a fragrant aroma.

If squash or pumpkin is not available, rutabaga makes a very good substitute.

Preheat the oven to 375°F/190°C. Heat the oil in a large, flameproof casserole. Add the chicken pieces and fry until golden brown, turning frequently.

Using a sharp knife, slice the onion, then peel and dice the pumpkin and seed and slice the bell pepper.

Drain any excess fat from the casserole and add the onion, pumpkin, and bell pepper. Gently fry for a few minutes until lightly browned. Add the chopped gingerroot, tomatoes, stock, and lentils. Season lightly with garlic salt and cayenne pepper.

Cover the casserole and cook in the preheated oven for 1 hour, or until the vegetables are tender and the chicken juices run clear when a skewer is inserted into the thickest part of the meat.

Add the drained corn and cook for an additional 5 minutes. Taste and adjust the seasoning, if necessary, then serve with crusty bread.

garlic chicken casserole

serves 4

20 minutes

2 hours 20 minutes

4 tbsp corn oil

2 lb/900 g chicken, chopped

9 oz/250 g mushrooms, sliced

16 shallots

6 garlic cloves, crushed

1 tbsp all-purpose flour

generous 1 cup white wine

generous 1 cup Chicken Stock
 (see page 5)

1 bouquet garni (1 bay leaf, 1 fresh
 thyme sprig, 1 celery stalk, 1 fresh
 parsley sprig, and 1 fresh sage sprig
 tied together with string)

salt and pepper

14 oz/400 g canned cranberry or
 cannellini beans

freshly cooked pattypan squash,
 to serve

*This is a cassoulet with a twist—
it is made with chicken instead
of duck and lamb. Save time
by using canned beans, such
as cranberry or cannellini beans,
which are both good in this dish.*

cook's tip

*Mushrooms are ideal in a
lowfat diet because they are
high in flavor and contain no fat.
Experiment with the wealth of
varieties that are now available
from supermarkets.*

*Serve the casserole with brown rice
to make this filling dish go
even further.*

Preheat the oven to 300°F/150°C. Heat the oil in a large, flameproof casserole. Add the chicken and fry until browned all over. Remove the chicken from the casserole with a slotted spoon and reserve until required.

Add the mushrooms, shallots, and garlic to the casserole and cook for 4 minutes.

Return the chicken to the casserole and sprinkle with the flour, then cook for an additional 2 minutes.

Add the wine and stock, stir until boiling, then add the bouquet garni. Season well with salt and pepper.

Drain the beans and rinse thoroughly, then add to the casserole.

Cover and place in the center of the preheated oven for 2 hours. Remove and discard the bouquet garni and serve the casserole with pattypans.

old english chicken

stewed in ale

serves 4–6

30 minutes

1 hour 45 minutes

4 large, skinless chicken thighs
2 tbsp all-purpose flour
2 tbsp English mustard powder
2 tbsp corn oil
1 tbsp butter
4 small onions
2½ cups beer
2 tbsp Worcestershire sauce
3 tbsp chopped fresh sage leaves
salt and pepper

rarebit toasts

½ cup freshly grated sharp Cheddar
   cheese
1 tsp English mustard powder
1 tsp all-purpose flour
1 tsp Worcestershire sauce
1 tbsp beer
2 slices whole-wheat toast
freshly cooked vegetables, to serve

This is a slow-cooked, old-fashioned stew to warm up a wintery day. The Rarebit Toasts are a perfect accompaniment to soak up the rich juices, but if you prefer, serve the stew with jacket potatoes.

cook's tip

If you do not have fresh sage, use 2 teaspoons dried sage instead.

Trim any excess fat from the chicken and toss in the flour and mustard powder to coat evenly. Heat the oil and butter in a large, flameproof casserole. Add the chicken and fry over fairly high heat, turning occasionally, until golden brown. Remove the chicken from the casserole with a slotted spoon and keep hot.

Slice the onions into wedges, then add to the casserole and fry quickly until golden brown. Add the chicken, beer, Worcestershire sauce, 1 tablespoon of the sage, and salt and pepper to taste. Bring to a boil, then cover and simmer very gently for 1½ hours, or until the chicken is very tender.

Meanwhile, make the Rarebit Toasts. Preheat the broiler to medium. Mix the cheese, mustard powder, flour, Worcestershire sauce, and beer together in a bowl. Spread the mixture over the toasts and cook under the hot broiler for 1 minute, or until melted and golden. Cut into triangles.

Stir the remaining sage leaves into the chicken stew, bring to a boil, and serve with the Rarebit Toasts and a selection of freshly cooked vegetables.

brittany chicken
casserole

serves 6

30 minutes

2 hours 40 minutes

1 lb 2 oz/500 g dried beans, such as
   flageolets, soaked overnight
   and drained
2 tbsp butter
2 tbsp olive oil
3 rindless bacon strips, chopped
2 lb/900 g chicken pieces
1 tbsp all-purpose flour

1¼ cups hard cider
⅔ cup Chicken Stock
   (see page 5)
salt and pepper
14 shallots
2 tbsp clear honey, warmed
8 oz/225 g cooked beets

*A hearty, one-dish meal that would
make a substantial lunch or supper.
As it requires a long cooking time,
make double quantities and freeze
half to eat later.*

cook's tip

*To save time, use canned flageolet
beans instead of dried. Drain and
rinse before adding to the chicken.*

Preheat the oven to 325°F/160°C. Cook the beans in salted boiling water
for 25 minutes, then drain thoroughly.

Heat the butter and oil in a large, flameproof casserole. Add the bacon
and chicken and cook for 5 minutes.

Sprinkle with the flour, then add the hard cider and stock, stirring constantly
to avoid lumps forming. Season to taste with salt and pepper and bring to
a boil.

Add the drained beans, then cover the casserole tightly and bake in
the center of the preheated oven for 2 hours, or until the chicken is very
tender.

About 15 minutes before the end of cooking time, uncover the casserole.

Gently cook the shallots and honey together in a skillet for 5 minutes,
turning the shallots frequently.

Add the shallots and cooked beets to the casserole and let finish cooking
in the oven for the last 15 minutes.

rich mediterranean chicken casserole

serves 4

30 minutes

1 hour 20 minutes

8 boneless chicken thighs

2 tbsp olive oil

1 red onion, sliced

2 garlic cloves, crushed

1 large red bell pepper, seeded and thickly sliced

thinly pared rind and juice of 1 small orange

½ cup Chicken Stock (see page 5)

14 oz/400 g canned chopped tomatoes

1 oz/25 g sun-dried tomatoes, thinly sliced

1 tbsp chopped fresh thyme

⅓ cup pitted black olives

salt and pepper

to garnish

orange rind

fresh thyme sprigs

fresh crusty bread, to serve

A colorful casserole packed with sunshine flavors from the Mediterranean. Sun-dried tomatoes add a wonderful richness and you need very few to make this dish really special.

cook's tip

Sun-dried tomatoes have a dense texture and concentrated taste, and add intense flavor to slow-cooking casseroles.

Fry the chicken without fat in a large, heavy-bottomed or nonstick skillet over fairly high heat, turning occasionally, until golden brown. Using a slotted spoon, drain off any excess fat from the chicken and transfer to a large, flameproof casserole.

Heat the oil in the skillet. Add the onion, garlic, and bell pepper and fry over medium heat for 3–4 minutes. Transfer to the casserole.

Add the orange rind and juice, stock, canned tomatoes, and sun-dried tomatoes and stir to mix.

Bring to a boil, then cover the casserole and simmer very gently over low heat for 1 hour, stirring occasionally, until the chicken is tender. Add the chopped thyme and pitted black olives, then season to taste with salt and pepper.

Sprinkle orange rind and thyme sprigs over the casserole to garnish, and serve with crusty bread.

chicken madeira

"french-style"

serves 8

30 minutes

2 hours 30 minutes

2 tbsp butter
20 shallots
9 oz/250 g carrots, sliced
9 oz/250 g rindless bacon, chopped
9 oz/250 g white mushrooms
1 whole chicken, weighing about
   3 lb 5 oz/1.5 kg
generous 1¾ cups white wine

3 tbsp all-purpose flour, seasoned
generous 1¾ cups Chicken Stock
   (see page 5)
salt and pepper
1 bouquet garni envelope
²⁄₃ cup Madeira wine
mashed potatoes, to serve

Madeira is a fortified wine which can be used in both sweet and savory dishes. Here it adds a rich, full flavor to the casserole.

cook's tip

You can add any combination of herbs to this recipe—chervil is a popular herb in French cuisine, but add it at the end of cooking so that its delicate flavor is not lost. Other herbs that work well with chicken are parsley and tarragon.

Heat the butter in a large, flameproof casserole. Add the shallots, carrots, bacon, and mushrooms and fry for 3 minutes, stirring frequently. Transfer to a plate and reserve.

Add the chicken to the casserole and cook until browned all over. Add the reserved vegetables and bacon to the casserole.

Add the white wine and cook until the wine is nearly reduced.

Sprinkle with the seasoned flour, stirring to avoid lumps forming.

Add the stock, salt and pepper to taste, and the bouquet garni. Cover and cook the casserole for 2 hours, or until the chicken is tender and the juices run clear when a skewer is inserted into the thickest part of the meat. About 30 minutes before the end of cooking time, add the Madeira wine and continue cooking uncovered.

Just before serving, remove and discard the bouquet garni. Carve the chicken and serve with mashed potatoes.

springtime chicken cobbler

serves 4

30 minutes

1 hour 25 minutes

1 tbsp oil

8 skinless chicken drumsticks

1 small onion, sliced

12 oz/350 g baby carrots

2 baby turnips

generous 1 cup fresh or frozen peas
   or fava beans

1 tsp cornstarch

1 1/4 cups Chicken Stock
   (see page 5)

2 bay leaves

salt and pepper

cobbler topping

1 3/4 cups whole-wheat all-purpose
   flour

2 tsp baking powder

2 tbsp soft sunflower margarine

2 tsp dry whole-grain mustard

2 oz/55 g Cheddar cheese, grated

2–3 tbsp skim milk, plus extra
   for brushing

sesame seeds, for sprinkling

Fresh spring vegetables are the basis of this colorful casserole, which is topped with hearty whole-wheat dumplings for a complete, healthy family meal.

Preheat the oven to 400°F/200°C. Heat the oil in a large skillet. Add the chicken and fry, turning frequently, until golden brown. Drain well and transfer to a large, flameproof casserole. Add the onion to the skillet and sauté for 2–3 minutes to soften.

Cut the carrots and turnips into equal-size pieces. Add to the casserole with the onion and peas or fava beans.

Blend the cornstarch with a little of the stock in a small pan, then stir in the remainder and heat gently, stirring, until boiling. Pour into the casserole and add the bay leaves and salt and pepper to taste. Cover and bake in the pre-heated oven for 50–60 minutes, or until the chicken is tender and the juices run clear when a skewer is inserted into the thickest part of the meat.

For the topping, sift the flour and baking powder into a large bowl, then mix in the margarine with a fork. Stir in the mustard, cheese, and enough milk to form a fairly soft dough. Roll out and cut out 16 rounds with a 1 1/2-inch/4-cm cookie cutter. Uncover the casserole, arrange the rounds on top, then brush with milk and sprinkle with sesame seeds. Bake in the oven for an additional 20 minutes, or until the topping is golden and firm.

californian chicken

serves 4–6

30 minutes

35–40 minutes

1 1/4 cups all-purpose flour

1 tsp paprika

1 tsp freeze-dried Italian seasoning

1 tsp freeze-dried tarragon

1 tsp fresh rosemary, finely crushed

salt and pepper

2 eggs, beaten

1/2 cup milk

1 whole chicken, weighing about 4 lb 8 oz/2 kg, jointed

3 tbsp all-purpose flour, seasoned

generous 3/4 cup corn oil

2 bananas, quartered

1 apple, cut into rings

12 oz/350 g canned corn and bell peppers, drained

to serve

crisp salad

peppercorn or horseradish sauce

It is better if you have time to bone the chicken completely, or use chicken breast after removing all the fat and skin.

Preheat the oven to 400°F/200°C. Mix the flour, paprika, herbs, and a pinch of salt together in a large bowl. Make a well in the center and mix in the beaten eggs.

Gradually add the milk, beating until very smooth.

Coat the chicken pieces with the seasoned flour, then dip the chicken pieces into the batter mix.

Heat 2/3 cup of the oil in a large skillet. Add the chicken pieces and fry for 3 minutes, or until lightly browned all over. Transfer the chicken to a non-stick cookie sheet and reserve.

Dip the bananas and apple rings into the batter, then add to the skillet and fry for 2 minutes. Remove from the skillet and reserve.

Finally, toss the corn and bell peppers into the leftover batter.

Heat the remaining oil in a separate skillet. Drop in spoonfuls of the corn mixture to make flat patties. Cook for 4 minutes on each side. Remove from the skillet and keep warm with the apple and banana fritters.

Bake the chicken in the preheated oven for 25 minutes, or until golden brown and tender and the juices run clear when a skewer is inserted into the thickest part of the meat.

Arrange the chicken, corn fritters, and the apple and banana fritters with a crisp salad. Serve with a peppercorn or horseradish sauce.

chicken with pearl
onions & green peas

serves 4

20 minutes

1 hour

generous 1 cup pork fat
salt and pepper
4 tbsp butter
16 pearl onions or shallots
2 lb 4 oz/1 kg boneless
    chicken pieces

3 tbsp all-purpose flour
2½ cups Chicken Stock
    (see page 5)
1 bouquet garni envelope
4½ cups fresh peas

Pork fat adds a tasty flavor to this dish. If you can't find fresh garden peas, frozen peas are a good substitute.

Preheat the oven to 400°F/200°C. Cut the pork fat into small cubes. Bring a pan of lightly salted water to a boil. Add the pork fat cubes and simmer for 3 minutes. Drain and dry the pork on paper towels.

Melt the butter in a large skillet. Add the pork fat and onions and fry gently for 3 minutes, or until lightly browned.

Remove the pork fat and onions from the skillet and reserve until required. Add the chicken pieces to the skillet and cook until browned all over. Transfer the chicken to a large, flameproof casserole.

Add the flour to the skillet and cook, stirring, until it begins to brown, then slowly blend in the stock.

Pour the sauce over the chicken and add the bouquet garni. Cook in the preheated oven for 35 minutes, or until the chicken is tender and the juices run clear when a skewer is inserted into the thickest part of the meat.

cook's tip

If you want to cut down on the fat, use lean bacon, cut into small cubes, rather than pork fat.

Remove and discard the bouquet garni about 10 minutes before the end of the cooking time and stir in the peas and reserved pork fat and onions. Taste and adjust the seasoning, if necessary.

To serve, place the chicken pieces on a large platter, surrounded by the pork, peas, and onions.

festive apple chicken

serves 6

30 minutes

2 hours

1 whole chicken, weighing about
    4 lb 8 oz/2 kg
sunflower oil, for brushing
2 dessert apples
1 tbsp butter
1 tbsp red currant jelly

stuffing
1 tbsp butter
1 small onion, finely chopped
2 oz/55 g mushrooms, finely chopped
2 oz/55 g smoked ham, finely
    chopped
$^1/_2$ cup fresh bread crumbs
1 tbsp chopped fresh parsley
1 crisp dessert apple
1 tbsp lemon juice
salt and pepper
freshly cooked mixed vegetables,
    to serve

The richly flavored stuffing in this recipe is cooked under the breast skin of the chicken, so not only is all the flavor sealed in, but the chicken stays really moist and succulent during cooking.

Preheat the oven to 375°F/190°C. To make the stuffing, melt the butter in a small pan. Add the onion and fry gently, stirring constantly, until softened but not browned. Stir in the mushrooms and cook for 2–3 minutes. Remove the pan from the heat and stir in the ham, bread crumbs, and chopped parsley.

Core the apple, leaving the skin on, and grate coarsely. Transfer to a small bowl and add the stuffing mixture and lemon juice. Season to taste with salt and pepper.

Loosen the breast skin of the chicken and carefully spoon the stuffing mixture under it, smoothing the skin over evenly with your hands.

Place the chicken in a roasting pan and brush lightly with oil.

Roast the chicken in the preheated oven for 25 minutes per 1 lb 2 oz/ 500 g plus 25 minutes, or until the chicken is tender and the juices run clear when a skewer is inserted into the thickest part of the meat. If the breast begins to brown too much, cover the chicken with foil.

Core and slice the remaining apples. Melt the butter in a skillet. Add the sliced apple and sauté until golden. Stir in the red currant jelly and warm through until melted. Garnish the chicken with the apple slices and serve with mixed vegetables.

roast chicken with
cilantro

serves 4–6

15 minutes, plus
4 hours chilling

2 hours

3 fresh cilantro sprigs, chopped
4 garlic cloves
½ tsp salt
1 tsp pepper, plus extra for sprinkling
4 tbsp lemon juice

4 tbsp olive oil
1 whole chicken, weighing about
   4 lb 8 oz/2 kg
fresh parsley sprig, to garnish
freshly cooked vegetables, to serve

In this recipe the chicken is coated with a fresh-flavored marinade, then roasted. Try serving it with rice, plain yogurt, and salad.

Place the cilantro, garlic, salt, pepper, lemon juice, and oil in a mortar and pound together with a pestle. Alternatively, transfer to a food processor and process until blended. Transfer to a nonmetallic bowl and let chill for 4 hours.

Preheat the oven to 375°F/190°C. Place the chicken in a roasting pan. Coat generously with the cilantro mixture. Sprinkle with pepper and roast in the preheated oven on a low shelf for 1½ hours, basting every 20 minutes with the cilantro mixture, until the chicken is tender and the juices run clear when a skewer is inserted into the thickest part of the meat. If the chicken begins to turn brown, cover with foil. Garnish with parsley and serve with freshly cooked vegetables.

cook's tip

For pounding small quantities, it is best to use a pestle and mortar so as little as possible of the mixture is left in the container.

variation

Any fresh herb can be used in this recipe instead of the cilantro. Tarragon or thyme are a good combination with chicken.

feta chicken with
mountain herbs

serves 4

20 minutes

40–45 minutes

8 skinless, boneless chicken thighs

2 tbsp each chopped fresh thyme, rosemary, and oregano

4¹/₂ oz/125 g feta cheese

salt and pepper

1 tbsp milk

2 tbsp all-purpose flour

fresh thyme, rosemary, and oregano leaves, to garnish

tomato sauce

1 tbsp olive oil

1 onion, coarsely chopped

1 garlic clove, crushed

4 plum tomatoes, quartered

fresh thyme, rosemary, and oregano sprigs

salt and pepper

Chicken goes well with most savory herbs, especially during the summer, when fresh herbs are at their best. This combination makes a good partner for tangy feta cheese and sun-ripened tomatoes.

Preheat the oven to 375°F/190°C. Spread out the chicken thighs on a cutting board, smooth-side downward.

Divide the herbs between the chicken thighs, then cut the cheese into 8 sticks. Place one stick of cheese in the center of each chicken thigh. Season well with salt and pepper, then roll up to enclose the cheese.

Place the rolls in an ovenproof dish, brush with milk, and dust with flour to coat evenly.

Bake in the preheated oven for 25–30 minutes, or until the chicken is tender and the juices run clear when a skewer is inserted into the thickest part of the meat.

To make the sauce, heat the oil in a small pan. Add the onion and garlic and cook, stirring, until softened and beginning to brown.

Add the tomatoes, reduce the heat, cover, and let simmer gently for 15–20 minutes, or until soft.

Add the herbs, then transfer to a food processor or blender and blend to a purée. Press through a strainer to make a smooth, rich sauce and season to taste. Slice the chicken and serve with the sauce, garnished with herbs.

squab chickens with
dried fruits

serves 2

20 minutes, plus
30 minutes soaking

25–30 minutes

3/4 cup dried apples, peaches, and
  prunes
1/2 cup boiling water
2 squab chickens
1/4 cup walnut halves
1 tbsp clear honey

1 tsp ground allspice
1 tbsp walnut oil
salt and pepper
freshly cooked vegetables, to serve

Squab chickens are ideal for a one- or two-portion meal, and cook very easily and quickly for a special dinner. If you're cooking for one, a microwave makes cooking even quicker and more convenient.

cook's tip

Alternative dried fruits that can be used in this recipe are cherries, mangoes, or papaya.

Place the dried fruits in a bowl, cover with the boiling water, and let soak for 30 minutes.

Preheat the oven to 375°F/190°C. Leave the squab chickens whole or cut in half, if you prefer.

Mix the fruits and any juices remaining in the bowl with the walnut halves, honey, and allspice, then divide the mixture between 2 small roasting bags or squares of foil.

Brush the chickens with the walnut oil and season to taste with salt and pepper, then place on top of the fruits.

Fold the foil over or close the roasting bags to seal the chickens in and place on a cookie sheet. Bake in the preheated oven for 25–30 minutes, or until the chickens are tender and the juices run clear when a skewer is inserted into the thickest part of the meat. To cook in a microwave, use microwave roasting bags and cook on High for 6–7 minutes each, depending on size.

Serve hot with freshly cooked vegetables.

chicken with
marmalade stuffing

serves 6

30 minutes

2 hours–2 hours 30 minutes

1 whole chicken, weighing about
  5 lb/2.25 kg
bay leaves
corn oil, for brushing

stuffing
1 tbsp corn oil
1 celery stalk, finely chopped
1 small onion, finely chopped
2½ cups fresh bread crumbs
4 tbsp marmalade
2 tbsp chopped fresh parsley

1 egg, beaten
salt and pepper

sauce
2 tsp cornstarch
2 tbsp orange juice
3 tbsp marmalade
⅔ cup Chicken Stock
  (see page 5)
1 orange
2 tbsp brandy
new potatoes, to serve

Marmalade lovers will enjoy this festive recipe. You can use any favorite marmalade, such as lemon or grapefruit.

Preheat the oven to 375°F/190°C. Lift the neck flap of the chicken and remove the wishbone using a small, sharp knife. Place a few bay leaves inside the body cavity.

For the stuffing, heat the oil in a pan. Add the celery and onion and sauté to soften. Add the bread crumbs, 3 tablespoons of the marmalade, the parsley, and egg. Season to taste with salt and pepper and use to stuff the neck cavity of the chicken. Any extra stuffing may be cooked separately.

Place the chicken in a roasting pan and brush lightly with oil. Roast in the preheated oven for 20 minutes per 1 lb 2 oz/500 g plus 20 minutes, or until the chicken is tender and the juices run clear when a skewer is inserted into the thickest part of the meat. Glaze with the remaining marmalade.

Meanwhile, to make the sauce, blend the cornstarch in a pan with the orange juice, then add the marmalade and stock. Heat gently, stirring, until thickened and smooth. Remove from the heat. Cut the segments from the orange, discarding all the white pith and membrane. Just before serving, add the orange segments and brandy to the sauce and bring to a boil.

Serve the chicken with the sauce, any extra stuffing, and new potatoes.

 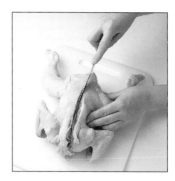 

golden chicken with mango & cranberries

serves 6

30 minutes

1 hour 30 minutes–2 hours

1 whole chicken, weighing about 5 lb/2.25 kg
6 rindless smoked bacon strips

stuffing

1 ripe mango, diced
1/2 cup fresh or frozen cranberries
2 1/2 cups fresh bread crumbs
1/2 tsp ground mace
1 egg, beaten
salt and pepper

glaze

1/2 tsp ground turmeric
2 tsp clear honey
2 tsp corn oil
seasonal vegetables, to serve

This recipe, which uses a part-boned chicken, is easy to slice and serve. If you prefer, stuff in the traditional way at the neck end, and cook any remaining stuffing separately.

Preheat the oven to 375°F/190°C. To part-bone the chicken, dislocate the legs and place the chicken breast-side downward. Cut a straight line through the skin along the ridge of the back. Scrape the meat down from the bone on both sides.

When you reach the point where the legs and wings join the body, cut through the joints, then work around the ribcage until the carcass can be lifted away.

Roll up the bacon and reserve. For the stuffing, mix the diced mango, cranberries, bread crumbs, and mace together in a bowl, then stir in the egg to bind the mixture. Season to taste with salt and pepper.

Place the chicken skin-side down and spoon over half of the stuffing. Arrange the bacon rolls down the center, then top with the remaining stuffing. Fold the skin over and tie with string. Turn the chicken over, truss the legs, and tuck the wings underneath. Place in a roasting pan. To make the glaze, mix the turmeric, honey, and oil together. Brush over the skin.

Roast in the oven for 1 1/2–2 hours, or until the chicken is tender and the juices run clear when a skewer is inserted into the thickest part of the meat. If the chicken begins to brown, cover with foil. Serve with vegetables.

roast chicken breasts with bacon

serves 8

15 minutes

30 minutes

4 tbsp butter
juice of 1 lemon
2¼ cups red currants or cranberries
1–2 tbsp raw brown sugar
salt and pepper
8 chicken suprêmes or breasts

16 lean bacon strips
1–2 tbsp chopped fresh thyme
4 tbsp beef drippings
4 slices bread, cut into triangles

Chicken suprêmes have a little bit of the wing bone remaining, which makes them easy to pick up and eat. In this recipe, a tart, fruity sauce perfectly complements the chicken and fried bread triangles.

cook's tip

You can use either chopped fresh thyme or dried thyme in this recipe, but remember that dried herbs have a stronger flavor so you only need half the quantity compared with fresh herbs.

Preheat the oven to 400°F/200°C. Heat the butter in a pan. Add the lemon juice, fruits, sugar, and salt and pepper to taste. Cook for 1 minute, then remove the pan from the heat and let cool until required.

Meanwhile, season the chicken with salt and pepper. Wrap 2 bacon strips around each breast and sprinkle with thyme.

Wrap each breast in a piece of lightly greased foil and place in a roasting pan. Roast in the preheated oven for 15 minutes. Remove the foil and roast for an additional 10 minutes, or until the chicken is tender and the juices run clear when a skewer is inserted into the thickest part of the meat.

Heat the drippings in a skillet. Add the bread triangles and fry on both sides until golden brown.

Arrange the triangles on a large serving plate and top each with a chicken breast. Serve with a spoonful of the fruit sauce.

pollo catalan

serves 8

20 minutes

1 hour 30 minutes

1 cup fresh brown bread crumbs
½ cup pine nuts
1 small egg, beaten
4 tbsp chopped fresh thyme or
   1 tbsp dried thyme
4 fresh peaches or 8 canned
   peach halves

salt and pepper
1 whole chicken, weighing about
   5 lb 8 oz/2.5 kg
1 tsp ground cinnamon
generous ¾ cup Amontillado sherry
4 tbsp heavy cream

The Catalan region of Spain is famous for its wonderful combinations of meat with fruits. In this recipe, peaches lend a touch of sweetness, and pine nuts, cinnamon, and sherry add an unusual twist.

Preheat the oven to 375°F/190°C. Mix the bread crumbs, half of the pine nuts, the egg, and thyme together in a bowl.

Halve and pit the peaches, removing the skin if necessary. Dice one peach into small pieces and stir into the bread crumb mixture. Season well with salt and pepper. Spoon the stuffing into the neck cavity of the chicken, securing the skin firmly over it.

Place the chicken in a roasting pan, then sprinkle the cinnamon over the skin. Cover loosely with foil and roast in the preheated oven for 1 hour, basting occasionally.

Remove the foil and spoon the sherry over the chicken. Cook for an additional 30 minutes, basting with the sherry, until the chicken is tender and the juices run clear when a skewer is inserted into the thickest part of the meat.

Sprinkle the remaining pine nuts over the remaining peach halves and place in an ovenproof dish. Cook in the oven for the last 10 minutes of the cooking time.

Transfer the chicken to a serving plate and arrange the peach halves around it. Skim any fat from the juices, stir in the cream, and heat gently. Serve with the chicken.

cook's tip

Canned apricot halves in natural juice make an easy pantry alternative.

suprême of chicken
with black cherries

serves 6

**20 minutes, plus
48 hours marinating**

40 minutes

6 large chicken suprêmes or breasts
6 black peppercorns, crushed
10½ oz/300 g fresh pitted black
   cherries or canned pitted cherries
   with their juice
12 shallots, sliced
4 rindless lean bacon strips, chopped
8 juniper berries

4 tbsp port
⅔ cup red wine
salt and pepper
2 tbsp butter
2 tbsp walnut oil
3 tbsp all-purpose flour
freshly cooked vegetables, to serve

*This recipe is rather time-
consuming, but it is well
worth the effort. Cherries
and chicken make a good
flavor combination.*

Place the chicken in a large ovenproof dish. Add the peppercorns, cherries and their juice (if using), and the shallots.

Add the bacon, juniper berries, port, and red wine. Season well with salt and pepper.

Let the chicken marinate in the refrigerator for 48 hours.

Preheat the oven to 350°F/180°C. Heat the butter and oil in a large skillet. Remove the chicken from the marinade, reserving the marinade in the dish, and add to the skillet. Fry quickly for 4 minutes on each side.

Return the chicken to the marinade, reserving the butter, oil, and juices in the skillet.

Cover the chicken with foil and bake in the preheated oven for 20 minutes. Transfer the chicken to a warm serving dish. Add the flour to the juices in the skillet and cook for 4 minutes. Add the marinade and bring to a boil, then simmer for 10 minutes, or until the sauce reaches a smooth consistency.

Pour the sauce over the chicken and serve with freshly cooked vegetables.

whisky roast chicken

serves 6

20 minutes

1 hour 40 minutes

1 whole chicken, weighing about
   4 lb 8 oz/2 kg
oil, for brushing
1 tbsp heather honey
2 tbsp Scotch whisky
2 tbsp all-purpose flour
1¼ cups Chicken Stock
   (see page 5)

stuffing

1 tbsp butter or corn oil

1 onion, finely chopped
1 celery stalk, thinly sliced
1 tsp dried thyme
4 tbsp porridge oats
4 tbsp Chicken Stock
   (see page 5)
salt and pepper

to serve

freshly cooked broccoli
sautéed potatoes

An unusual change from a plain roast, with a distinctly warming Scottish flavor and a delicious oatmeal stuffing.

Preheat the oven to 375°F/190°C. To make the stuffing, heat the butter in a small pan. Add the onion and celery and fry over medium heat, stirring constantly, until softened and lightly browned.

Remove the pan from the heat and stir in the thyme, oats, stock, and salt and pepper to taste.

Stuff the neck end of the chicken with the mixture and tuck the neck flap under. Place in a roasting pan, brush lightly with oil, and roast in the pre-heated oven for 1 hour.

Mix the heather honey with 1 tablespoon of the whisky and brush the mixture over the chicken. Return to the oven for an additional 20 minutes, or until the chicken is golden brown and the juices run clear when a skewer is inserted into the thickest part of the meat.

Transfer the chicken to a large serving plate. Skim the fat from the juices remaining in the roasting pan, then stir in the flour. Stir over medium heat until the mixture begins to bubble, then gradually add the stock and remaining whisky.

Bring to a boil, stirring, then simmer for 1 minute. Serve the chicken with the sauce, broccoli, and sautéed potatoes.

roast chicken in exotic
mushroom sauce

serves 4

30 minutes, plus
2 hours chilling

1 hour 50 minutes

6 tbsp butter, softened
1 garlic clove, crushed
salt and pepper
1 large chicken, weighing about
    4 lb 8 oz/2 kg
6 oz/175 g exotic mushrooms
12 shallots
3 tbsp all-purpose flour

^{2}/3 cup brandy, warmed
1^1/4 cups heavy cream
1 tbsp chopped fresh parsley,
    to garnish

to serve

roast potatoes
lightly cooked green beans

*This unusual chicken dish has
the flavor of roast chicken, but
is finished off in a casserole with
an exotic mushroom sauce.*

Place the butter, garlic, and salt and pepper to taste in a bowl and mix well.

Rub the mixture inside and outside of the chicken and let chill in the refrigerator for 2 hours.

Preheat the oven to 450°F/230°C. Place the chicken in a large roasting pan and roast in the center of the preheated oven for 1½ hours, basting with the garlic butter every 10 minutes.

Remove the chicken from the roasting pan and let cool slightly.

Transfer the chicken juices to a pan, add the mushrooms and shallots, and cook for 5 minutes. Sprinkle with the flour. Add the warm brandy and light with a taper or long match.

When the flames die down, add the cream and cook for 3 minutes on very low heat, stirring constantly.

Reduce the oven temperature to 325°F/160°C. Cut the chicken into small bite-size pieces, then place in a casserole. Cover with the mushroom sauce and bake in the oven for an additional 12 minutes. Garnish with parsley and serve with roast potatoes and green beans.

honeyed citrus chicken

serves 4

30 minutes, plus
4 hours chilling

40–45 minutes

1 whole chicken, weighing about
    4 lb 8 oz/2 kg
salt and pepper

marinade

1¼ cups orange juice
3 tbsp cider vinegar
3 tbsp clear honey
2 tbsp chopped fresh tarragon
2 oranges, cut into wedges

sauce

handful of fresh tarragon sprigs,
    chopped
scant 1 cup ricotta cheese
2 tbsp orange juice
1 tsp clear honey
⅓ cup stuffed olives, chopped
fresh tarragon sprigs, to garnish

*This lowfat recipe is great
for summer entertaining served
simply with a green salad and new
potatoes. If you cut the chicken in
half and press it flat, you can roast
it in under an hour.*

Place the chicken on a cutting board, breast-side downward. Cut through the bottom part of the carcass using poultry shears or heavy kitchen scissors, making sure not to cut right through to the breastbone below.

Rinse the chicken with cold water, drain, and place on a clean cutting board with the skin-side uppermost. Press the chicken flat, then cut off the leg ends.

Thread 2 long wooden skewers diagonally through the bird from each breast to the opposite leg, to keep it flat. Season the skin to taste with salt and pepper.

Place all the marinade ingredients, except the orange wedges, in a shallow, nonmetallic dish. Mix, then add the chicken. Cover and let chill in the refrigerator for 4 hours, turning the chicken several times.

To make the sauce, mix all the ingredients together and season. Spoon into a serving dish, cover, and chill until required.

Preheat the oven to 400°F/200°C. Transfer the chicken and marinade to a roasting pan, open out the chicken, and place skin-side downward. Tuck the orange wedges around the chicken and roast in the preheated oven for 25 minutes. Turn the chicken over and roast for an additional 20–30 minutes, basting frequently, or until the chicken is browned and the juices run clear when a skewer is inserted into the thickest part of the meat. Garnish with tarragon sprigs and serve with the sauce.

breast of chicken with ham & blue cheese

serves 4

20 minutes

45 minutes

4 boneless chicken breasts
8 fresh sage leaves
salt and pepper
8 thin slices lean cooked ham
9 oz/250 g blue cheese, cut into 8 slices
8 rindless lean bacon strips

²⁄₃ cup Chicken Stock (see page 5)
2 tbsp port
24 shallots
1 lb 2 oz/500 g baby beets, cooked
1 tbsp cornstarch, blended with a little port

Beets are one of the most underrated vegetables, adding flavor and color to numerous dishes. Tender young beets are used in this recipe.

cook's tip

English Stilton is perfect for this dish, but if you can't find it, try Gorgonzola or Roquefort.

Preheat the oven to 375°F/190°C. Cut a long slit horizontally along each chicken breast to make a pocket.

Insert 2 sage leaves into each pocket and season to taste with salt and pepper.

Wrap each slice of ham around a slice of cheese and place 2 into each chicken pocket. Carefully wrap enough bacon around each breast to completely cover the pockets containing the ham and the cheese.

Place the breasts in an ovenproof dish and pour over the stock and port.

Add the shallots, cover with a lid or foil, and braise in the preheated oven for 40 minutes, or until the chicken is tender and the juices run clear when a skewer is inserted into the thickest part of the meat.

Carefully place each breast on a cutting board and slice through them to create a fan effect. Serve them on a warm serving dish with the shallots and beets.

Place the juices from the casserole in a pan and bring to a boil, then remove from the heat and add the cornstarch paste. Simmer for 2 minutes, then pour over the shallots and beets.

springtime roast chicken

serves 4

20 minutes

I hour I0 minutes

5 tbsp fresh brown bread crumbs
generous ¾ cup sour cream
5 tbsp chopped fresh parsley
5 tbsp snipped fresh chives
salt and pepper
4 squab chickens
I tbsp corn oil

I lb 8 oz/675 g young spring
  vegetables such as carrots,
  zucchini, sugar snap peas, baby
  corn, and turnips, cut into
  small chunks
½ cup boiling Chicken Stock
  (see page 5)
2 tsp cornstarch
⅔ cup dry white wine

Squab chickens are simple to prepare, take about 30 minutes to roast, and can be easily cut in half lengthwise with a sharp knife. One squab chicken makes a substantial serving for each person.

Preheat the oven to 425°F/220°C. Mix the bread crumbs, one-third of the sour cream, and 2 tablespoons each of the parsley and chives together in a bowl. Season well with salt and pepper, then spoon into the neck ends of the chickens. Place the chickens in a roasting pan, brush with oil, and season well.

Roast in the preheated oven for 30–35 minutes, or until the chickens are tender and the juices run clear when a skewer is inserted into the thickest part of the meat.

Place the vegetables in a shallow, ovenproof dish in a single layer and add half the remaining herbs with the stock. Cover and bake in the oven for 25–30 minutes, or until tender. Strain the vegetables, reserving the cooking juices, and keep warm.

Transfer the chickens to a serving plate and skim any fat from the juices in the pan. Add the reserved vegetable juices to the juices in the pan.

Blend the cornstarch with the wine and whisk into the sauce with the remaining sour cream. Whisk until boiling, then add the remaining herbs. Season to taste. Spoon the sauce over the chickens and serve immediately with the vegetables.

boned chicken
with parmesan

 serves 6

 40 minutes

 1 hour 30 minutes

1 whole chicken, weighing about
   5 lb/2.25 kg
8 slices mortadella or salami
2¼ cups fresh white or brown bread
   crumbs
generous 1 cup freshly grated
   Parmesan cheese

2 garlic cloves, crushed
6 tbsp chopped fresh basil or parsley
pepper
1 egg, beaten
olive oil, for brushing
freshly cooked spring vegetables,
   to serve

*It's really very easy to bone
a whole chicken, but if you
prefer, you can ask a friendly
butcher to do this for you.*

Preheat the oven to 400°F/200°C. Bone the chicken, keeping the skin intact. Dislocate each leg by breaking it at the thigh joint. Cut down each side of the backbone, taking care not to pierce the breast skin.

Pull the backbone clear of the flesh and discard. Remove the ribs, severing any attached flesh with a sharp knife.

Scrape the flesh from each leg and cut away the bone at the joint with a knife or poultry shears.

Use the bones for stock. Lay out the boned chicken on a cutting board, skin-side down. Arrange the mortadella or salami slices over the chicken, overlapping slightly.

Place the bread crumbs, Parmesan, garlic, and basil in a bowl. Season well with pepper and mix together. Stir in the beaten egg to bind the mixture. Pile the mixture down the center of the boned chicken, roll the meat around it, and tie securely with fine cotton string.

variation

*Replace the mortadella
with lean bacon
strips, if you prefer.*

Place in a roasting dish and brush lightly with olive oil. Roast in the preheated oven for 1½ hours, or until the chicken is tender and the juices run clear when a skewer is inserted into the thickest part of the meat.

Serve hot or cold, in slices, with freshly cooked spring vegetables.

chicken with creamy
zucchini stuffing

serves 6

20 minutes

1 hour 30 minutes–2 hours

1 whole chicken, weighing about
   5 lb/2.25 kg
corn oil, for brushing
9 oz/250 g zucchini
2 tbsp butter
juice of 1 lime

stuffing

3 oz/85 g zucchini
6 tbsp medium-fat soft cheese
finely grated rind of 1 lime
2 tbsp fresh bread crumbs
salt and pepper

A cheesy stuffing is tucked under the breast skin of the chicken to give added flavor and moistness to the meat.

cook's tip

For quicker cooking, finely grate the zucchini rather than cutting them into strips.

Preheat the oven to 375°F/190°C. To make the stuffing, coarsely grate the zucchini. Transfer to a bowl, add the cheese, lime rind, and bread crumbs and mix together. Season to taste with salt and pepper.

Carefully ease the skin away from the breast of the chicken. Push the stuffing under the skin with your fingers, to cover the breast evenly.

Place the chicken in a baking pan, brush with oil, and roast in the preheated oven for 20 minutes per 1 lb 2 oz/500 g plus 20 minutes, or until the chicken is tender and the juices run clear when a skewer is inserted into the thickest part of the meat.

Meanwhile, cut the remaining zucchini into long, thin ribbons with a potato peeler or sharp knife. Melt the butter in a skillet. Add the zucchini and lime juice and sauté until just tender. Serve with the chicken.

pot roast orange & sesame chicken

serves 4

15 minutes

2 hours

2 tbsp corn oil
1 whole chicken, weighing about
   3 lb 5 oz/1.5 kg
2 large oranges
2 small onions, quartered
1 lb 2 oz/500 g small, whole carrots
   or thin carrots, cut into
   2-inch/5-cm lengths

salt and pepper
2/3 cup orange juice
2 tbsp brandy
2 tbsp sesame seeds
1 tbsp cornstarch
1 tbsp water

This colorful, nutritious pot roast could be served for a family meal or for a special dinner. Add more vegetables if you're feeding a crowd—if your roasting pot is large enough!

variation

Use lemons instead of oranges for a sharper citrus flavor and place a fresh thyme sprig in the chicken cavity with the lemon half as they are a good flavor combination.

Preheat the oven to 375°F/190°C. Heat the oil in a large, heavy-bottomed pan. Add the chicken and fry, turning occasionally, until evenly browned.

Cut one orange in half and place one half inside the chicken cavity. Place the chicken in a large, deep casserole. Arrange the onions and carrots around the chicken.

Season well with salt and pepper and pour over the orange juice.

Cut the remaining oranges into thin wedges and tuck around the chicken in the casserole, among the vegetables.

Cover and cook in the preheated oven for 1½ hours, or until the vegetables and chicken are tender and the juices run clear when a skewer is inserted into the thickest part of the meat. Uncover and sprinkle with the brandy and sesame seeds, then return to the oven for 10 minutes.

To serve, transfer the chicken to a large platter. Place the vegetables around the chicken. Skim any excess fat from the juices in the casserole. Blend the cornstarch with the water, then stir into the juices and bring to a boil, stirring constantly. Season to taste with salt and pepper, then serve the sauce with the chicken.

honey & mustard
baked chicken

serves 4–6

15 minutes

30 minutes

8 chicken pieces
4 tbsp butter, melted
4 tbsp mild mustard
4 tbsp clear honey
2 tbsp lemon juice

1 tsp paprika
salt and pepper
3 tbsp poppy seeds
tomato and corn salad, to
serve (optional)

*Chicken pieces are brushed
with a classic combination of
honey and mustard, then a crunchy
coating of poppy seeds is added.*

cook's tip

*Mexican rice makes an excellent
accompaniment. Boil the rice for
10 minutes, drain, then fry for
5 minutes. Add chopped onions,
garlic, tomatoes, carrots, and chile
and cook for 1 minute before
adding ²/₃ cup stock. Bring to a boil,
cover, and cook for 20 minutes,
adding more stock if necessary.
Add peas 5 minutes before the end
of the cooking time.*

Preheat the oven to 400°F/200°C. Place the chicken, skinless-side down, on a large cookie sheet.

Place all the other ingredients, except the poppy seeds, in a large bowl and blend together well.

Brush the mixture over the chicken.

Bake in the center of the preheated oven for 15 minutes.

Carefully turn the chicken over and coat the top side with the remaining honey and mustard mixture.

Sprinkle the chicken with poppy seeds and return to the oven for an additional 15 minutes, or until the chicken is tender and the juices run clear when a skewer is inserted into the thickest part of the meat.

Arrange the chicken on a serving plate, pour over the cooking juices, and serve with a tomato and corn salad, if you like.

mediterranean-style
sunday roast

serves 6

15 minutes

2 hours

1 whole chicken, weighing about
   5 lb 8 oz/2.5 kg
fresh rosemary sprigs
6 oz/175 g feta cheese,
   coarsely grated
2 tbsp sun-dried tomato paste
4 tbsp butter, softened
salt and pepper
1 garlic bulb

2 lb 4 oz/1 kg new potatoes, halved
   if large
1 each red, green, and yellow bell
   pepper, seeded and cut into
   chunks
3 zucchini, thinly sliced
2 tbsp olive oil
2 tbsp all-purpose flour
2¹/₂ cups Chicken Stock
   (see page 5)

*A roast that is full of
Mediterranean flavor.
A mixture of feta cheese,
rosemary, and sun-dried
tomatoes is stuffed under
the chicken skin, then
roasted with garlic, new
potatoes, and vegetables.*

Preheat the oven to 375°F/190°C. Rinse the chicken inside and out with cold water and drain well. Carefully cut between the skin and the top of the breast meat using a small pointed knife. Slide a finger into the slit and carefully enlarge it to form a pocket. Continue until the skin is completely lifted away from both breasts and the top of the legs.

Chop the leaves from 3 rosemary sprigs. Place the feta, sun-dried tomato paste, butter, and pepper to taste in a bowl. Add the rosemary leaves and mix together, then spoon under the skin of the chicken.

Place the chicken in a large roasting pan, cover with foil, and cook in the preheated oven for 20 minutes per 1 lb 2 oz/500 g plus 20 minutes, or until the chicken is tender and the juices run clear when a skewer is inserted into the thickest part of the meat.

Break the garlic bulb into cloves, but do not peel. Add to the chicken with the vegetables after 40 minutes. Drizzle with oil, tuck in a few rosemary sprigs, and season well with salt and pepper. Cook for the remaining time, removing the foil for the last 40 minutes to brown the chicken.

Transfer the chicken to a serving plate. Place some of the vegetables around the chicken and transfer the remainder to a serving dish. Skim any excess fat from the juices, then stir in the flour. Cook for 2 minutes, then gradually stir in the stock. Bring to a boil, stirring, until thickened. Strain into a sauceboat and serve with the chicken.

cheddar baked chicken

serves 4

10 minutes

30–35 minutes

1 tbsp milk

2 tbsp English mustard

1/2 cup freshly grated sharp Cheddar cheese

3 tbsp all-purpose flour

2 tbsp snipped fresh chives

4 skinless, boneless chicken breasts

to serve

jacket potatoes

mixed salad

Cheese and mustard, and a simple, crispy coating, make a delicious combination for this healthy dish.

cook's tip

There are several varieties of mustard available. For a sharper flavor, try French varieties—Meaux mustard has a grainy texture with a warm, spicy flavor, while Dijon mustard is medium-hot and tangy.

It is a good idea to freeze herbs as they retain their color, flavor, and nutrients very well. Chives are particularly suitable for freezing— store them in labeled plastic bags and shake them dry before use. Dried chives are a poor substitute for fresh.

Preheat the oven to 400°F/200°C. Mix the milk and mustard together in a bowl. Mix the cheese, flour, and chives together in a separate bowl.

Dip the chicken breasts into the milk and mustard mixture, brushing to coat evenly.

Dip the chicken breasts into the cheese mixture, pressing to coat evenly. Place on a cookie sheet and spoon any extra cheese coating over the top.

Bake in the preheated oven for 30–35 minutes, or until golden brown and the juices run clear when a skewer is inserted into the thickest part of the meat. Serve the chicken hot with jacket potatoes and a mixed salad.

gardener's chicken

serves 4

15 minutes, plus
30 minutes cooling

1 hour 40 minutes

9 oz/250 g parsnips, chopped
4$\frac{1}{2}$ oz/125 g carrots, chopped
$\frac{1}{2}$ cup fresh bread crumbs
$\frac{1}{4}$ tsp grated nutmeg
1 tbsp chopped fresh parsley
salt and pepper
1 whole chicken, weighing about
   3 lb 5 oz/1.5 kg
bunch of fresh parsley

$\frac{1}{2}$ onion
2 tbsp butter, softened
4 tbsp olive oil
1 lb 2 oz/500 g new potatoes,
   scrubbed
1 lb 2 oz/500 g baby carrots
chopped fresh parsley, to garnish

*Any combination of small, young
vegetables, such as zucchini,
leeks, and onions, can be
roasted with the chicken.*

Place the parsnips and carrots in a large pan, half cover with water, and bring to a boil. Cover and simmer until tender. Drain well, then transfer to a food processor or blender and process to a purée. Transfer the purée to a bowl and let cool.

Mix in the bread crumbs, nutmeg, and parsley and season to taste with salt and pepper.

Preheat the oven to 375°F/190°C. Place the stuffing in the neck end of the chicken and push a little under the skin over the breast meat. Secure the flap of skin with a small metal skewer or toothpick.

Place the bunch of parsley and onion inside the cavity of the chicken, then place the chicken in a large roasting pan.

Spread the butter over the skin and season to taste with salt and pepper, cover with foil, and roast in the preheated oven for 30 minutes.

Meanwhile, heat the oil in a skillet. Add the potatoes and cook until lightly browned.

Transfer the potatoes to the roasting pan and add the baby carrots. Baste the chicken and continue to cook for an additional hour, or until the chicken is tender and the juices run clear when a skewer is inserted into the thickest part of the meat. Baste the chicken and vegetables after 30 minutes.

Remove the foil for the last 20 minutes to allow the skin to crisp. Garnish the vegetables with chopped parsley and serve.

barbecues & grills

There is nothing more delicious than the juicy flesh and charred skin of chicken that has been barbecued over an open fire—after marinating in a flavorful mixture of oil and herbs or spices. Try an Asian-style mixture of yogurt and aromatic spices, or soy sauce, sesame oil, and fresh gingerroot. There are some unusual flavors and innovative tastes, including Skewered Chicken with Bramble Sauce (see page 214), and Skewered Chicken Spirals (see page 220), which are attractive whirls of chicken, bacon, and basil. Squab chickens, flavored with lemon and tarragon in this section, are perfect for broiling or barbecuing. There is also a recipe for Broiled Chicken & Vegetable Salad (see page 198), which combines chicken breasts with a selection of broiled vegetables including zucchini, eggplant, and red bell pepper drizzled with olive oil and served with crusty bread to soak up the delicious juices.

chicken cajun-style

serves 4

10 minutes, plus
1 hour marinating

15–20 minutes

16 chicken wings
4 tsp paprika
2 tsp ground coriander
1 tsp celery salt
1 tsp ground cumin
1/2 tsp cayenne pepper
1/2 tsp salt

1 tbsp corn oil
2 tbsp red wine vinegar
fresh parsley sprigs, to garnish

to serve

cherry tomatoes
mixed salad greens
sauce of your choice

These spicy chicken wings are good served with a chili salsa and salad. Alternatively, if this is too spicy for your taste, try a sour cream and chive dip.

Rinse the chicken wings with cold water and pat dry with paper towels. Remove the wing tips with kitchen scissors.

Mix the paprika, coriander, celery salt, cumin, cayenne pepper, salt, oil, and red wine vinegar together in a small bowl.

Rub this mixture over the wings to coat evenly and let marinate in the refrigerator for at least 1 hour.

Preheat the barbecue. Cook the chicken wings over hot coals, brushing occasionally with oil and turning frequently, for 15 minutes, or until the juices run clear when a skewer is inserted into the thickest part of the meat. Garnish with fresh parsley and serve with cherry tomatoes, mixed salad greens, and a sauce of your choice.

cook's tip

To save time, you can buy ready-made Cajun spice seasoning to rub over the chicken wings.

variation

Although chicken wings do not have much meat on them, they are small and easy to pick up with your fingers, which makes them ideal for barbecues. However, they can also be enjoyed fried or roasted.

spicy sesame chicken

serves 4

10 minutes

12–15 minutes

4 chicken quarters
²/₃ cup plain yogurt
finely grated rind and juice of
  1 small lemon
2 tsp medium-hot curry paste
1 tbsp sesame seeds

to serve
mixed salad greens
naan bread
lemon wedges

This is a quick and easy recipe for the broiler, perfect for lunch or to eat outdoors on a picnic.

Preheat the broiler to medium. Remove the skin from the chicken and make cuts in the flesh at intervals with a sharp knife.

Mix the yogurt, lemon rind, lemon juice, and curry paste together in a bowl to form a smooth mixture.

Spoon the mixture over the chicken and arrange on a foil-lined broiler pan or cookie sheet.

Place the chicken quarters under the hot broiler and broil for 12–15 minutes, turning once, or until golden brown and tender and the juices run clear when a skewer is inserted into the thickest part of the meat. Just before the end of the cooking time, sprinkle the chicken with the sesame seeds.

Serve with mixed salad greens, naan bread, and lemon wedges.

cook's tip

If you have time, leave the chicken and the sauce in the refrigerator to marinate overnight so the flavors are fully absorbed.

variation

Poppy seeds, fennel seeds, or cumin seeds, or a mixture of all three, can also be used to sprinkle over the chicken.

ginger chicken & corn

serves 6

10 minutes

15–20 minutes

3 fresh corn cobs
12 chicken wings
1-inch/2.5-cm piece fresh gingerroot
6 tbsp lemon juice
4 tsp corn oil
1 tbsp golden superfine sugar

to serve
jacket potatoes
mixed salad greens

Chicken wings and corn in a sticky ginger marinade are designed to be eaten with the fingers—there's no other way!

cook's tip

Cut off the wing tips before broiling as they burn very easily. Alternatively, you can cover them with small pieces of foil.

When you are buying fresh corn, look for plump, tightly packed kernels. If fresh corn is unavailable, you can use thawed, frozen corn instead.

Preheat the broiler to medium. Remove the husks and silken hairs from the corn. Using a sharp knife, cut each cob into 6 slices. Place in a large bowl with the chicken wings.

Peel and grate the fresh gingerroot or finely chop.

Mix the ginger, lemon juice, oil, and sugar together in a bowl, then pour over the corn and chicken and toss until evenly coated.

Thread the corn and chicken wings on to 6 metal skewers, to make turning easier.

Cook the corn and chicken under the hot broiler for 15–20 minutes, basting with the gingery glaze and turning frequently, or until the corn is golden brown and tender and the chicken is cooked through. Alternatively, cook on a barbecue over hot coals. Serve with jacket potatoes and a salad.

broiled chicken & vegetable salad

serves 4

10 minutes, plus
1 hour standing/marinating

25–30 minutes

1 small eggplant, sliced
salt and pepper
2 garlic cloves, crushed
finely grated rind of ½ lemon
1 tbsp chopped fresh mint
6 tbsp olive oil, plus extra for
   brushing and drizzling
4 boneless chicken breasts

2 zucchini, sliced
1 red bell pepper, seeded
   and quartered
1 small fennel bulb, thickly sliced
1 large red onion, thickly sliced
1 small ciabatta loaf or 1 French
   baguette, sliced

Broiling is a quick, healthy cooking method, ideal for sealing in the juices and flavor of chicken breasts, and a wonderful way to cook summer vegetables.

Place the eggplant slices in a colander and sprinkle with salt. Let drain over a bowl for 30 minutes, then rinse and pat dry with paper towels. This will get rid of any bitter juices.

Mix the garlic, lemon rind, mint, and olive oil together in a small bowl, then season to taste with salt and pepper.

Slash the chicken breasts at intervals with a sharp knife and place in a large bowl. Spoon over about half of the oil mixture and stir until coated.

Mix the eggplant and remaining vegetables together in a separate bowl, then toss in the remaining oil mixture and stir to mix. Cover and let the chicken and vegetables marinate in the refrigerator for 30 minutes.

Preheat the broiler to medium. Arrange the chicken breasts and vegetables on a broiler pan and cook under the hot broiler, turning occasionally, until they are golden brown and tender and the juices run clear when a skewer is inserted into the thickest part of the meat. Alternatively, cook on a ridged grill pan on the stove.

Brush the bread slices with olive oil and broil until golden.

Drizzle a little olive oil over the chicken and broiled vegetables and serve hot or cold with the toasts.

tropical chicken skewers

serves 6

10 minutes

8–10 minutes

1 lb 10 oz/750 g boneless
  chicken breasts
2 tbsp medium sherry
pepper
3 mangoes

bay leaves
2 tbsp corn oil
2 tbsp coarsely shredded coconut
crisp salad, to serve

In this recipe, chicken is given a Caribbean flavor. The marinade keeps it moist and succulent during cooking.

cook's tip

Remember that if you are using metal skewers they will get very hot, so be sure to use gloves or tongs to turn them. Wooden skewers should be soaked in water for 30 minutes before use to prevent them burning under the broiler, and the exposed ends should be covered with pieces of foil.

Use mangoes that are ripe but still firm so that they hold together on the skewers during cooking. Another firm fruit that would be suitable is pineapple.

Preheat the broiler to medium. Remove the skin from the chicken, cut into 1-inch/2.5-cm cubes, and toss in the sherry, with a little pepper.

Using a sharp knife, cut the mangoes into 1-inch/2.5-cm cubes, discarding the pits and skins.

Thread the chicken, mango cubes, and bay leaves alternately on to long metal skewers, then brush lightly with oil.

Cook under the hot broiler for 8–10 minutes, turning occasionally, until golden brown and the chicken is cooked through.

Sprinkle the skewers with the coconut and broil for an additional 30 seconds. Serve with a crisp salad.

sweet & sour
drumsticks

serves 4

10 minutes, plus
1 hour marinating

20 minutes

8 chicken drumsticks
4 tbsp red wine vinegar
2 tbsp tomato paste
2 tbsp soy sauce
2 tbsp clear honey

1 tbsp Worcestershire sauce
1 garlic clove, crushed
good pinch of cayenne pepper
fresh parsley sprig, to garnish
crisp salad, to serve

Chicken drumsticks are marinated to impart a tangy, sweet and sour flavor and a shiny glaze.

Skin the chicken, if desired, and slash 2–3 times with a sharp knife. Arrange the chicken drumsticks in a single layer in a shallow, nonmetallic container.

Mix the red wine vinegar, tomato paste, soy sauce, honey, Worcestershire sauce, garlic, and cayenne pepper together in a small bowl and pour over the chicken drumsticks.

Cover and let marinate in the refrigerator for 1 hour. Preheat the barbecue. Cook the drumsticks over the hot coals for 20 minutes, brushing with the marinade and turning during cooking, or until the chicken is tender and the juices run clear when a skewer is inserted into the thickest part of the meat. Garnish with parsley and serve with a crisp salad.

cook's tip

For an extra tangy flavor, add the juice of 1 lime to the marinade. While the drumsticks are cooking, check regularly to ensure that they are not burning.

variation

This sweet and sour marinade would also work well with pork or shrimp. Thread pork cubes or shrimp on to skewers with bell peppers and shallots.

chicken with
garden herbs

serves 4

10 minutes, plus
1 hour 30 minutes
cooling/chilling

25–30 minutes

4 part-boned, skinless chicken breasts

6 tbsp olive oil

2 tbsp lemon juice

4 tbsp finely chopped fresh summer
  herbs, such as parsley, chives,
  and mint

pepper

1 ripe avocado

generous $\frac{1}{2}$ cup mascarpone cheese

cold cooked rice, to serve

*Warm weather calls for lighter
eating, and this chilled chicken
dish in a subtle herb vinaigrette is
ideal for a summer dinner party,
or for a picnic.*

cook's tip

*To remove the pit easily from
an avocado, first cut the avocado
in half. Holding one half securely
in your hand, tap the knife into
the pit so that it becomes
embedded, then carefully twist
the knife to dislodge the pit.*

*The chicken can be cooked several
hours in advance and stored in the
refrigerator until required.*

Preheat the broiler to medium. Using a sharp knife, cut 3–4 deep slashes in the chicken breasts.

Place the chicken in a large, flameproof dish and brush lightly with a little of the olive oil.

Cook the chicken under the hot broiler, turning once, until golden brown and the juices run clear when a skewer is inserted into the thickest part of the meat.

Mix the remaining oil, lemon juice, and herbs together, then season with pepper to taste. Spoon the oil mixture over the chicken and let cool, then cover and let chill in the refrigerator for 1 hour.

Remove the pit from the avocado (see Cook's Tip) and place the flesh in a food processor or blender with the mascarpone cheese and process to a purée. Season to taste with pepper. Serve the chicken with the avocado sauce and rice.

skewered spicy tomato chicken

serves 4

10 minutes

8–10 minutes

1 lb 2 oz/500 g skinless, boneless chicken breasts

3 tbsp tomato paste

2 tbsp clear honey

2 tbsp Worcestershire sauce

1 tbsp chopped fresh rosemary

9 oz/250 g cherry tomatoes

fresh rosemary sprigs, to garnish

freshly cooked couscous or rice, to serve

These lowfat, spicy skewers are cooked in a matter of minutes. In addition, they can be assembled ahead of time and stored in the refrigerator until you need them.

cook's tip

Couscous is made from semolina that has been made into separate grains. It is very easy to prepare— simply soak it in a bowl of boiling water and then fluff up the grains with a fork. Flavorings such as lemon or nutmeg can be added.

Cherry tomatoes are ideal for barbecues as they can be threaded straight on to skewers. As they are kept whole, the skins keep in the tomatoes' natural juices.

Preheat the broiler to medium. Using a sharp knife, cut the chicken into 1-inch/2.5-cm chunks and place in a bowl.

Mix the tomato paste, honey, Worcestershire sauce, and chopped rosemary together in a separate bowl. Add to the chicken, stirring to coat evenly.

Thread the chicken pieces and tomatoes alternately on to 8 presoaked wooden skewers, then spoon over any remaining glaze.

Cook under the hot broiler for 8–10 minutes, turning occasionally, until the chicken is cooked through. Serve on a bed of couscous or rice and garnish with rosemary sprigs.

broiled chicken with pesto toasts

serves 4

10 minutes

20 minutes

8 part-boned chicken thighs
olive oil, for brushing
1¼ cups strained tomatoes
½ cup green or red
    pesto sauce

12 slices French bread
¾ cup freshly grated
    Parmesan cheese
½ cup pine nuts or slivered almonds
salad greens, to serve

This Italian-style dish is richly flavored with pesto, which is a mixture of basil, olive oil, pine nuts, and Parmesan cheese. Either red or green pesto can be used for this recipe.

cook's tip

Although leaving the skin on the chicken means that it will have a higher fat content, many people like the rich taste and crispy skin, especially when it is blackened by the broiler. The skin also keeps in the cooking juices.

Preheat the broiler to medium. Arrange the chicken in a single layer in a wide, flameproof dish and brush lightly with oil. Cook under the hot broiler for 15 minutes, turning occasionally, until golden brown.

Pierce the chicken with a skewer to ensure that there is no trace of pink in the juices.

Pour off any excess fat. Warm the strained tomatoes and half the pesto sauce in a small pan and pour over the chicken. Broil for an additional few minutes, turning, until coated.

Meanwhile, spread the remaining pesto on to the slices of bread. Arrange the bread over the chicken and sprinkle with the Parmesan cheese. Scatter the pine nuts over the cheese. Broil for 2–3 minutes, or until browned and bubbling. Serve the chicken with the toasts and salad greens.

mustardy barbecue drummers

serves 4

10 minutes

25–30 minutes

10 smoked lean bacon strips
1 garlic clove, crushed
3 tbsp whole-grain mustard
4 tbsp fresh brown bread crumbs

8 chicken drumsticks
1 tbsp corn oil
fresh parsley sprigs, to garnish

Great for barbecues, or for simple summer lunches and picnics, this is an easy and tasty recipe for chicken drumsticks.

cook's tip

Don't cook the chicken over the hottest part of the barbecue or the outside may be charred before the center is cooked.

Preheat the broiler to medium or preheat the barbecue. Chop 2 of the bacon strips into small pieces and fry in a skillet without fat for 3–4 minutes, stirring constantly. Remove the skillet from the heat and stir in the crushed garlic, 2 tablespoons of the whole-grain mustard, and the bread crumbs.

Carefully loosen the skin from each drumstick with your fingers, being careful not to tear the skin. Spoon a little of the mustard stuffing under each flap of skin, smoothing the skins over firmly afterward.

Wrap a bacon strip around each drumstick, and secure with toothpicks.

Mix the remaining mustard and oil together, then brush over the chicken drumsticks. Cook over the hot coals or under the hot broiler for 25 minutes, or until the chicken is tender and the juices run clear when a skewer is inserted into the thickest part of the meat.

Garnish with parsley sprigs. The drumsticks may be served hot or cold.

minty lime chicken

serves 6

10 minutes, plus
30 minutes marinating

25–30 minutes

3 tbsp finely chopped fresh mint
4 tbsp clear honey
4 tbsp lime juice
12 boneless chicken thighs

sauce
²/₃ cup plain thick yogurt
1 tbsp finely chopped fresh mint
2 tsp finely grated lime rind
mixed salad, to serve

These tangy lime and honey-coated pieces have a matching sauce or dip based on creamy plain yogurt. They could be served at a barbecue or as an entrée for a dinner party.

Mix the mint, honey, and lime juice together in a bowl.

Use toothpicks to keep the chicken thighs in neat shapes and place in a large, nonmetallic bowl. Add the marinade to the chicken and turn to coat evenly.

Cover and let marinate in the refrigerator for at least 30 minutes, or preferably overnight. Preheat the barbecue or preheat the broiler to medium. Cook the chicken over the hot coals or under the hot broiler, turning frequently and basting with the marinade, until the chicken is tender and the juices run clear when a skewer is inserted into the thickest part of the meat.

Meanwhile, mix the sauce ingredients together.

Remove the toothpicks from the chicken and serve with the sauce and a mixed salad.

cook's tip

Mint can be grown very easily in a backyard or window box. It is a useful herb for marinades and salad dressings. Other useful herbs to grow are parsley and basil.

variation

Use this marinade for chicken kabobs, alternating the chicken with lime and red onion wedges.

skewered chicken with bramble sauce

serves 4

10 minutes

12–15 minutes

4 chicken breasts or 8 thighs
4 tbsp dry white wine or hard cider
2 tbsp chopped fresh rosemary
pepper
¼ tsp grated nutmeg

sauce

1½ cups blackberries, plus extra
   to garnish
1 tbsp cider vinegar
2 tbsp red currant jelly
fresh rosemary sprigs, to garnish
green salad, to serve

*The tart flavor of blackberries
makes them an ideal fruit for use in
savory dishes, and they are
particularly good with chicken. Their
color makes an impact, too!*

Using a sharp knife, cut the chicken into 1-inch/2.5-cm pieces and place in
a bowl. Sprinkle over the white wine and rosemary and season well with
pepper. Cover and let marinate in the refrigerator for at least 1 hour.

Preheat the broiler to medium. Drain the chicken, reserving the marinade,
and thread the meat on to 8 metal or presoaked wooden skewers.

Cook under the hot broiler for 8–10 minutes, turning occasionally, until
golden and cooked through.

Meanwhile, to make the sauce, place the marinade in a small pan with the
blackberries and simmer gently until soft. Press the mixture through a
strainer using the back of a spoon.

Return the blackberry purée to the pan with the cider vinegar and red
currant jelly and bring to a boil. Boil, uncovered, until the sauce is reduced
by about one-third.

cook's tip

*If you use canned fruits,
omit the red currant jelly.*

Spoon a little bramble sauce on to each plate and place a chicken skewer
on top. Sprinkle with nutmeg, garnish with rosemary and blackberries, and
serve with a green salad.

broiled squab chickens
with lemon & tarragon

serves 2

15 minutes

35 minutes

2 squab chickens
salt and pepper
4 fresh tarragon sprigs, plus extra
    to garnish
1 tsp corn oil

2 tbsp butter
grated rind of ½ lemon
1 tbsp lemon juice
1 garlic clove, crushed
orange slices, to garnish
new potatoes, to serve

Butterflied squab chickens are complemented by the delicate fragrance of lemon and tarragon and broiled.

Preheat the broiler to medium. To prepare the chickens, turn them breast-side down on a cutting board and cut them through the backbone using kitchen scissors. Crush each bird gently to break the bones so that they lie flat while cooking. Season each with salt.

Turn them over and insert a tarragon sprig under the skin over each side of the breast.

Using a pastry brush, brush the chickens with oil and place under the hot broiler about 5 inches/13 cm from the heat. Broil the chickens for 15 minutes, turning halfway through, until they are lightly browned.

Meanwhile, to make the glaze, melt the butter in a small pan. Add the lemon rind, lemon juice, and garlic, then season to taste with salt and pepper.

cook's tip

Once the chickens are flattened, insert 2 metal skewers through them to keep them flat.

Brush the chickens with the glaze and cook for an additional 15 minutes, or until the juices run clear when a skewer is inserted into the thickest part of the meat, turning them once and brushing regularly so that they stay moist. Garnish with tarragon and orange slices and serve with new potatoes.

grilled chicken

quarters with warm aïoli

serves 4

15 minutes, plus
2 hours marinating

25–30 minutes

4 chicken quarters
2 tbsp corn oil
2 tbsp lemon juice
2 tsp dried thyme
salt and pepper
lemon slices, to garnish
green salad, to serve

aïoli

5 garlic cloves, crushed
pinch of salt
2 egg yolks
½ cup each olive oil and corn oil
2 tsp lemon juice
2 tbsp boiling water

Chicken quarters are grilled, then served with a strongly flavored garlic mayonnaise, which originated in Provence, France.

cook's tip

To make a quick aïoli, add the garlic to 1¼ cups good-quality mayonnaise, then place in a bowl set over a pan of warm water and beat together. Just before serving, add 1–2 tablespoons hot water.

Using a skewer, prick the chicken quarters in several places, then place them in a shallow nonmetallic dish.

Mix the oil, lemon juice, thyme, and seasoning together in a bowl, then pour over the chicken, turning to coat the chicken evenly. Cover and let marinate in the refrigerator for 2 hours.

Preheat the barbecue or preheat the broiler to medium. To make the aïoli, beat the garlic and salt together to form a paste. Add the egg yolks and beat well. Gradually add the oils, drop by drop, beating vigorously, until the mayonnaise becomes creamy and smooth. Continue to add the oils in a thin, steady trickle and beat until the aïoli is thick. Stir in the lemon juice and season with pepper to taste. Keep warm until required.

Place the chicken over the hot coals or under the hot broiler and cook, brushing with the marinade and turning the pieces to cook evenly, for 25–30 minutes, or until the juices run clear when a skewer is inserted into the thickest part of the meat. Transfer to a serving plate.

Beat the water into the aïoli and turn into a warm serving bowl. Serve the chicken with the aïoli and a green salad, garnished with lemon slices.

skewered chicken spirals

serves 4

10 minutes

10 minutes

4 skinless, boneless chicken breasts
1 garlic clove, crushed
2 tbsp tomato paste
4 smoked Canadian bacon strips

large handful of fresh basil leaves
salt and pepper
corn oil, for brushing
green salad, to serve

These unusual chicken kabobs have a wonderful Mediterranean flavor, and the bacon helps keep them moist during cooking.

Preheat the barbecue or preheat the broiler to medium. Spread out a chicken breast between 2 sheets of plastic wrap and beat firmly with a rolling pin to flatten the chicken to an even thickness. Repeat with the remaining breasts of chicken.

Mix the crushed garlic and tomato paste together until well blended. Spread the mixture evenly over the surface of the chicken.

Lay a bacon strip over each piece of chicken, then scatter with the fresh basil leaves. Season well with salt and pepper.

Roll up each piece of chicken firmly, then cut into thick slices using a sharp knife. Thread the slices securely on to 4 metal or presoaked skewers, making sure that the skewer holds the chicken in a spiral shape.

Brush the skewers lightly with oil and cook over the hot coals or under the hot broiler for 5 minutes, then turn the skewers over and cook for an additional 5 minutes, or until the chicken is cooked through. Serve with a green salad.

cook's tip

Flattening the chicken breasts makes them thinner so that they cook more quickly. It also makes them easier to roll.

variation

To complete the Mediterranean theme, serve these kabobs with Parmesan-topped garlic bread.

spicy dishes

Because chicken is popular throughout the world, there are countless spicy recipes from Asia, Mexico, the Caribbean, Spain, and Japan. Lime juice, peanut, coconut, and chile add the authentic tastes of Thailand to Chile Coconut Chicken (see page 254), while Kashmiri Chicken (see page 250) is a rich and spicy dish from Northern India with an aromatic sauce made from yogurt, Tikka curry paste, cumin, ginger, chili, and almonds. From Spain comes Spanish Chicken with Shrimp (see page 240) with its unusual mixture of chicken and shellfish, together with the famous spicy Spanish sausage, chorizo, slow-cooked in a sauce of garlic, tomatoes, and white wine. Cumin-Spiced Apricot Chicken (see page 252) is a creative modern dish that would be perfect for any special occasion. The chicken is stuffed with dried apricots, coated in a yogurt, cumin, and turmeric sauce, and served with nutty rice. There is even a dish from Japan, Teppanyaki (see page 236), a simple dish of fried chicken slices with bell peppers, scallions, and bean sprouts, served with a mirin dipping sauce.

chicken in red bell
pepper & almond sauce

serves 4

10 minutes

40–45 minutes

2 tbsp butter

7 tbsp vegetable oil

4 skinless, boneless chicken breasts, cut into 2-x-1-inch/ 5-x-2.5-cm pieces

1 onion, coarsely chopped

1-inch/2.5-cm piece fresh gingerroot

3 garlic cloves

¼ cup blanched almonds

1 large red bell pepper, seeded and coarsely chopped

1 tbsp ground cumin

2 tsp ground coriander

1 tsp ground turmeric

pinch of cayenne pepper

½ tsp salt

⅔ cup water

3 star anise

2 tbsp lemon juice

pepper

slivered almonds, to garnish

cooked rice, garnished with fresh flatleaf parsley leaves, to serve

This tasty chicken dish combines warm spices and almonds and is spiked with star anise.

Heat the butter and 1 tablespoon of the oil in a skillet. Add the chicken pieces and cook for 5 minutes, or until golden. Transfer the chicken pieces to a plate and keep warm until required.

Place the onion, gingerroot, garlic, almonds, red bell pepper, cumin, coriander, turmeric, cayenne pepper, and salt in a food processor or blender and process to a smooth paste.

Heat the remaining oil in a large pan or deep skillet. Add the paste and fry for 10–12 minutes.

Add the chicken pieces, the water, star anise, lemon juice, and pepper to taste. Cover, reduce the heat, and simmer gently for 25 minutes, or until the chicken is tender and cooked through, stirring occasionally during cooking.

Transfer the chicken to a serving dish, sprinkle with the slivered almonds, and serve with freshly cooked rice, garnished with parsley.

fruity garlic
curried chicken

serves 4–6

10 minutes

2 hours 20 minutes

1 tbsp corn oil

2 lb/900 g chicken, chopped

scant 1/2 cup all-purpose flour, seasoned

32 shallots, coarsely chopped

4 garlic cloves, crushed with a little olive oil

3 cooking apples, diced

1 pineapple, diced

generous 2/3 cup golden raisins

1 tbsp clear honey

1 1/4 cups Chicken Stock (see page 5)

2 tbsp Worcestershire sauce

3 tbsp hot curry paste

salt and pepper

2/3 cup sour cream

orange slices, to garnish

freshly cooked rice, to serve

Serve this fruity curry with mango chutney and naan bread, and top the curry with seedless grapes. Mangoes or pears make a good substitute for pineapple.

variation

Coconut rice also makes an excellent accompaniment. Place 1 oz/25 g chopped creamed coconut, 1 cinnamon stick, and 2 1/2 cups water in a large pan and bring to a boil. Stir in 1 3/4 cups basmati rice, cover, and simmer gently for 15 minutes, or until all the liquid has been absorbed. Discard the cinnamon stick.

Preheat the oven to 350°F/180°C. Heat the oil in a large skillet. Coat the chicken in the seasoned flour and cook for 4 minutes, or until browned all over. Transfer the chicken to a large, deep casserole and keep warm until required.

Gently fry the shallots, garlic, apples, pineapple, and golden raisins in the remaining pan drippings.

Add the honey, stock, Worcestershire sauce, and hot curry paste. Season to taste with salt and pepper.

Pour the sauce over the chicken and cover the casserole.

Cook in the center of the preheated oven for 2 hours. Stir in the sour cream and cook for an additional 15 minutes. Serve the curry with rice, garnished with orange slices.

spicy chicken tortillas

serves 4

15 minutes

30–35 minutes

2 tbsp corn oil

8 skinless, boneless chicken thighs, sliced

I onion, chopped

2 garlic cloves, chopped

I tsp cumin seeds, coarsely crushed

2 large dried chiles, sliced

14 oz/400 g canned tomatoes

14 oz/400 g canned red kidney beans, drained and rinsed

2/3 cup Chicken Stock (see page 5)

2 tsp sugar

salt and pepper

to serve

I large ripe avocado

I lime

8 soft tortillas

generous I cup plain thick yogurt

Serve these easy-to-prepare tortillas to friends or as a special family supper. The chicken filling has a mild, mellow spicy heat and a fresh salad makes a perfect accompaniment.

variation

For a vegetarian filling, replace the chicken with 14 oz/400 g canned pinto or cannellini beans and use vegetable stock instead of the Chicken Stock.

Heat the oil in a large skillet or preheated wok. Add the chicken and fry for 3 minutes, until golden. Add the onion and fry for 5 minutes, stirring, until browned. Add the garlic, cumin, and chiles and cook for 1 minute.

Add the tomatoes, kidney beans, stock, sugar, and salt and pepper to taste. Bring to a boil, breaking up the tomatoes. Cover and simmer for 15 minutes. Remove the lid and cook for 5 minutes, stirring occasionally, until the sauce has thickened.

Halve the avocado, discard the pit, and scoop out the flesh on to a plate. Mash the avocado with a fork. Cut half of the lime into 8 thin wedges and reserve. Squeeze the juice from the remaining lime over the avocado.

Warm the tortillas following the package instructions. Place 2 tortillas on each serving plate, fill with the chicken mixture, and top with spoonfuls of avocado and yogurt. Garnish the tortillas with the reserved lime wedges.

cajun chicken gumbo

serves 2

10 minutes

25–30 minutes

1 tbsp corn oil
4 chicken thighs
1 small onion, diced
2 celery stalks, diced
1 small green bell pepper, seeded and diced
scant $^1/_2$ cup long-grain rice

1 $^1/_4$ cups Chicken Stock (see page 5)
1 small, fresh red chile
9 oz/250 g okra
1 tbsp tomato paste
salt and pepper

This complete main course is cooked in one pan for simplicity. If you're cooking for one, simply halve the ingredients; the cooking time should stay the same.

Heat the oil in a large pan. Add the chicken and fry until golden. Remove the chicken from the pan using a slotted spoon. Stir in the onion, celery, and bell pepper and fry for 1 minute. Pour off any excess fat.

Add the rice and fry, stirring briskly, for an additional minute. Add the stock and heat until boiling.

Thinly slice the chile and trim the okra. Add to the pan with the tomato paste. Season to taste with salt and pepper.

Return the chicken to the pan and stir. Cover tightly and simmer gently for 15 minutes, or until the rice is tender, the chicken is thoroughly cooked, and all the liquid absorbed. Stir occasionally, and if the gumbo becomes too dry, add a little extra stock to moisten. Serve immediately.

cook's tip

The whole chile makes the dish hot and spicy—if you prefer a milder flavor, discard the seeds of the chile.

variation

You can replace the chicken with 9 oz/250 g shelled shrimp and 3 oz/85 g pork belly, if desired. Slice the pork and fry in the oil before adding the onions, and add the shrimp 5 minutes before the end of the cooking time.

mexican chicken

serves 4

10 minutes

40–45 minutes

2 tbsp oil
8 chicken drumsticks
1 onion, finely chopped
1 tsp chili powder
1 tsp ground coriander
14 oz/400 g canned chopped
    tomatoes

2 tbsp tomato paste
1 cup frozen corn
salt and pepper

to serve
freshly cooked rice
mixed bell pepper salad

Chiles, tomatoes, and corn are typical ingredients in a Mexican dish.

cook's tip

Mexican dishes are not usually suitable for freezing because the strong flavors they contain, such as chili, intensify during freezing, and if left for too long, an unpleasant, musty flavor can develop.

Heat the oil in a large skillet. Add the chicken drumsticks and cook over medium heat until lightly browned. Remove the chicken drumsticks from the skillet with a slotted spoon and reserve until required.

Add the chopped onion to the skillet and cook for 3–4 minutes, or until softened, then stir in the chili powder and coriander and cook for a few seconds, stirring constantly. Add the chopped tomatoes with their juice and the tomato paste and stir well to incorporate.

Return the chicken drumsticks to the skillet and simmer the casserole gently for 20 minutes, or until the chicken is tender and the juices run clear when a skewer is inserted into the thickest part of the meat. Add the corn and cook for an additional 3–4 minutes. Season to taste with salt and pepper.

Serve the chicken with rice and a mixed bell pepper salad.

chicken with bell peppers & black bean sauce

serves 4

10 minutes, plus
30 minutes standing

10 minutes

14 oz/400 g chicken breasts,
   thinly sliced

salt and pepper

pinch of cornstarch

2 tbsp corn oil

1 garlic clove, crushed

1 tbsp black bean sauce

1 each small red and green bell
   pepper, seeded and cut into strips

1 fresh red chile, finely chopped

2³⁄4 oz/75 g mushrooms, sliced

1 onion, chopped

6 scallions, chopped

1 tsp cornstarch, blended with a little
   rice wine

seasoning

¹⁄2 tsp salt

¹⁄2 tsp sugar

3 tbsp Chicken Stock
   (see page 5)

1 tbsp dark soy sauce

2 tbsp beef stock

2 tbsp rice wine

cooked fresh noodles, to serve

*This tasty chicken stir-fry is
quick and easy to make and
is full of fresh flavors and
crunchy vegetables.*

cook's tip

*Black bean sauce can be found
in specialty stores and in many
supermarkets. Use dried noodles
if you can't find fresh noodles.*

Place the chicken strips in a bowl. Add the salt and cornstarch and cover with water. Let stand for 30 minutes.

Heat 1 tablespoon of the oil in a preheated wok or skillet. Add the chicken and stir-fry for 4 minutes. Transfer the chicken to a serving dish and clean the pan.

Add the remaining oil to the pan and add the garlic, black bean sauce, green and red bell peppers, chile, mushrooms, onion, and scallions. Stir-fry the vegetables for 2 minutes, then return the chicken strips to the pan.

Add the seasoning ingredients, stir-fry for 3 minutes, then thicken with a little of the cornstarch paste. Serve with fresh noodles.

teppanyaki

serves 4

10 minutes

10–15 minutes

4 boneless chicken breasts
1 red bell pepper
1 green bell pepper
4 scallions
8 baby corn

3½ oz/100 g bean sprouts
1 tbsp corn oil
4 tbsp soy sauce
4 tbsp mirin
1 tbsp grated fresh gingerroot

This simple, Japanese style of cooking is ideal for thinly sliced breast of chicken. Mirin is a rich, sweet rice wine which is available from Asian food markets.

variation

If you cannot find mirin, add 1 tablespoon of brown sugar to the sauce instead.

Instead of serving the sauce as a dip, you could use it as a marinade. However, do not leave it to marinate for more than 2 hours, otherwise the soy sauce will cause the chicken to dry out and become tough. Use other vegetables, such as snow peas or thinly sliced carrots, if you prefer.

Using a sharp knife, remove the skin from the chicken and slice at a slight angle, to a thickness of about ¼ inch/5 mm.

Seed and thinly slice the bell peppers and trim and slice the scallions and baby corn. Arrange the bell peppers, scallions, baby corn, and bean sprouts on a plate with the sliced chicken.

Heat a large grill pan or heavy-based skillet, then lightly brush with oil. Add the vegetables and chicken slices in small batches, allowing space between them so that they cook thoroughly.

Mix the soy sauce, mirin, and gingerroot together in a small bowl and serve as a dip with the chicken and vegetables.

caribbean chicken

serves 4

10 minutes, plus
2 hours marinating

30–35 minutes

8 skinless chicken drumsticks
2 limes
1 tsp cayenne pepper
2 mangoes
1 tbsp corn oil

2 tbsp raw brown sugar
2 tbsp coarsely grated coconut
 (optional), for sprinkling

to garnish
lime wedges
fresh flatleaf parsley sprigs

*This exotic dish can be made
with any cut of chicken, but
drumsticks are best for quick and
even cooking. Grated fresh coconut
adds a delicious, tropical flavor.*

variation

*When buying mangoes, bear in
mind that the skin of ripe mangoes
varies in color from green to pinky-
red and the flesh from pale yellow
to bright orange. Choose mangoes
that yield to gentle pressure.*

Using a sharp knife, slash the chicken drumsticks at intervals, then place
them in a large nonmetallic bowl.

Grate the rind from the limes and reserve until required.

Squeeze the juice from the limes and sprinkle over the chicken with the
cayenne pepper. Cover and let marinate in the refrigerator for at least
2 hours, or preferably overnight.

Peel the mangoes and chop in half. Discard the pit and cut the flesh into
slices.

Drain the chicken drumsticks using a slotted spoon and reserve the
marinade. Heat the oil in a wide, heavy-bottomed skillet. Add the chicken
drumsticks and sauté, turning frequently, until golden. Stir in the marinade,
reserved lime rind, mango slices, and the sugar.

Cover the skillet and simmer gently, stirring occasionally, for 15 minutes, or
until the chicken is tender and the juices run clear when a skewer is
inserted into the thickest part of the meat. Sprinkle with grated coconut
(if using) and garnish with lime wedges and fresh parsley.

spanish chicken with shrimp

serves 4

10 minutes

1 hour

4 chicken quarters
1 tbsp olive oil
1 red bell pepper
1 onion
2 garlic cloves, crushed
14 oz/400 g canned chopped
   tomatoes
generous 3/4 cup dry white wine

4 tbsp chopped fresh oregano
salt and pepper
4 1/2 oz/125 g chorizo sausage
4 1/2 oz/125 g cooked, shelled shrimp
freshly cooked rice, to serve

This unusual dish, with its mixture of chicken and shellfish, is typically Spanish. The basis of this recipe is sofrito: a slow-cooked mixture of onion and tomato in olive oil, with garlic and bell peppers.

Using a sharp knife, remove the skin from the chicken quarters. Heat the oil in a wide, heavy-bottomed skillet. Add the chicken and fry, turning occasionally, until golden brown.

Using a sharp knife, seed and slice the bell pepper and onion. Add the bell pepper and onion to the skillet and fry gently to soften.

Add the garlic with the chopped tomatoes, wine, and oregano. Season well with salt and pepper, then bring to a boil. Cover and simmer gently for 45 minutes, or until the chicken is tender and the juices run clear when a skewer is inserted into the thickest part of the meat.

cook's tip

Chorizo is a spicy Spanish sausage made with pork and a hot pepper such as cayenne or pimento. It is available from large supermarkets and specialty butchers.

Thinly slice the chorizo and add to the skillet together with the shrimp, then simmer for an additional 5 minutes. Adjust the seasoning to taste and serve with freshly cooked rice.

chicken korma

serves 4–6

10 minutes, plus
3 hours 10 minutes
marinating/standing

40 minutes

1 lb 10 oz/750 g skinless chicken
1 ¼ cups heavy cream
½ tsp garam masala (see Cook's Tip)

korma paste

2 garlic cloves
1-inch/2.5-cm piece fresh gingerroot,
   coarsely chopped
⅓ cup blanched almonds
6 tbsp Chicken Stock
   (see page 5)

1 tsp ground cardamom
4 cloves, crushed
1 tsp cinnamon
2 large onions, chopped
1 tsp coriander seeds
2 tsp ground cumin
pinch of cayenne pepper
6 tbsp olive oil
salt and pepper
fresh cilantro sprigs, to garnish
freshly cooked rice, to serve

Korma is a typically mild and aromatic curry. If you want to reduce the fat in this recipe, use plain yogurt instead of the cream.

cook's tip

Garam masala is the name given to the mixture of spices used in curries. It can be bought ready-mixed or you can prepare your own. Grind 1 teaspoon cardamom seeds, 2 teaspoons cloves, 2 tablespoons each cumin seeds and coriander seeds, 3-inch/7.5-cm piece cinnamon stick, 1 tablespoon black peppercorns, and 1 dried red chile.

Place all the ingredients for the korma paste in a food processor or blender and process to a very smooth paste.

Cut the chicken into cubes, then place in a large bowl. Pour over the korma paste and stir to coat. Cover and let marinate in the refrigerator for 3 hours.

Transfer the chicken to a large pan and simmer in its own juices for 25 minutes, adding a little stock if the mixture becomes too dry.

Add the cream and garam masala to the pan and simmer for an additional 15 minutes, or until the chicken is cooked through. Remove the pan from the heat and let the korma stand for 10 minutes before serving. Garnish the chicken korma with fresh cilantro and serve with freshly cooked rice.

regal chicken with cashew nut stuffing

serves 4

15 minutes

1 hour 20 minutes

1 whole chicken, weighing about
 3 lb 5 oz/1.5 kg
1 small onion, halved
2 tbsp butter, melted, plus extra for
 greasing
1 tsp ground turmeric
1 tsp ground ginger
1/2 tsp cayenne pepper
salt and pepper

stuffing

2 tbsp corn oil
1 onion, finely chopped
1/2 medium red bell pepper, seeded
 and finely chopped

2 garlic cloves, crushed
2/3 cup basmati rice
1 1/2 cups hot Chicken Stock
 (see page 5)
grated rind of 1/2 lemon
1/2 tsp ground turmeric
1/2 tsp ground ginger
1/2 tsp ground coriander
pinch of cayenne pepper
generous 1/2 cup salted cashew nuts
pepper
fresh coriander sprigs, to garnish
gravy, to serve

*Most of the flavorful stuffing
is cooked separately from the
chicken; only a small amount
is added to the neck end.*

Preheat the oven to 375°F/190°C. To make the stuffing, heat the oil in a pan. Add the onion, red bell pepper, and garlic and cook gently for 4–5 minutes. Add the rice and stir to coat in the oil. Add the stock, bring to a boil, then simmer for 15 minutes, or until all the liquid is absorbed. Transfer to a bowl and add the remaining ingredients for the stuffing. Season well with pepper.

Place half the stuffing in the neck end of the chicken and secure with a toothpick. Place the halved onion into the cavity of the chicken. Spoon the rest of the stuffing into a greased ovenproof dish and cover with foil.

Place the chicken in a roasting pan. Prick all over with a fork, avoiding the stuffed area. Mix the butter and spices together in a bowl, season to taste with salt and pepper, then brush over the chicken.

Roast in the preheated oven for 1 hour, basting occasionally, until the chicken is tender and the juices run clear when a skewer is inserted into the thickest part of the meat. About 30 minutes before the end of the cooking time, place the dish of stuffing in the oven. Remove the toothpick, garnish the chicken with cilantro, and serve with the stuffing and gravy.

thai stir-fried chicken with vegetables

serves 4

10 minutes

8–10 minutes

3 tbsp sesame oil

12 oz/350 g chicken breast, thinly sliced

salt and pepper

8 shallots, sliced

2 garlic cloves, finely chopped

1-inch/2.5-cm piece fresh gingerroot, grated

1 fresh green chile, finely chopped

1 each red and green bell pepper, seeded and thinly sliced

3 zucchini, thinly sliced

2 tbsp ground almonds

1 tsp ground cinnamon

1 tbsp oyster sauce

1 3/4 oz/50 g creamed coconut, grated

Coconut adds a creamy texture and delicious flavor to this Thai-style stir-fry, which is spiked with green chile.

cook's tip

Creamed coconut is sold in blocks by supermarkets and Asian markets. It is a useful pantry standby as it adds richness and depth of flavor.

Since most of the heat of chiles comes from the seeds, remove them before cooking if you want a milder flavor. Be very careful when handling chiles—do not touch your face or eyes as the chile juice can be very painful. Always wash your hands after preparing chiles.

Heat the sesame oil in a preheated wok. Add the chicken, season to taste with salt and pepper, and stir-fry for 4 minutes.

Add the shallots, garlic, gingerroot, and chile and stir-fry for 2 minutes.

Add the bell peppers and zucchini and stir-fry for about 1 minute.

Finally, add the ground almonds, cinnamon, oyster sauce, and grated coconut, then taste and adjust the seasoning, if necessary. Stir-fry for an additional minute and serve immediately.

golden chicken pilau

serves 4

10 minutes

15–20 minutes

4 tbsp butter

8 skinless, boneless chicken thighs, cut into large pieces

1 onion, sliced

1 tsp ground turmeric

1 tsp ground cinnamon

1 1/4 cups long-grain rice

salt and pepper

1 3/4 cups plain yogurt

1/3 cup golden raisins

generous 3/4 cup Chicken Stock (see page 5)

1 tomato, chopped

2 tbsp chopped fresh cilantro or parsley

2 tbsp toasted coconut

fresh cilantro sprigs, to garnish

This is a simple version of a creamy textured and mildly spiced Indian pilau. Although there are lots of ingredients, there's very little preparation needed for this dish.

cook's tip

Long-grain rice is the most widely available and the cheapest rice. Basmati, with its slender grains and aromatic flavor, is more expensive and should be used on special occasions if it is not affordable on a frequent basis. Rice, especially basmati, should be washed thoroughly under cold running water before use.

Heat the butter in a heavy-bottomed or nonstick pan. Add the chicken and onion and fry for 3 minutes.

Stir in the turmeric, cinnamon, and rice, season to taste with salt and pepper, and fry gently for 3 minutes.

Add the yogurt, golden raisins, and stock and mix well. Cover and simmer for 10 minutes, stirring occasionally, until the rice and chicken are tender and all the stock has been absorbed. Add more stock if the mixture becomes too dry.

Stir in the chopped tomato and fresh cilantro.

Sprinkle the pilau with toasted coconut and garnish with fresh cilantro. Serve immediately.

kashmiri chicken

serves 4

10 minutes, plus
1 hour marinating

30 minutes

4 skinless chicken drumsticks
4 skinless chicken thighs
²⁄₃ cup plain yogurt
4 tbsp Tikka curry paste
2 tbsp corn oil
1 onion, thinly sliced
1 garlic clove, crushed

1 tsp ground cumin
1 tsp finely chopped fresh gingerroot
½ tsp chili paste
4 tsp Chicken Stock
  (see page 5)
2 tbsp ground almonds
salt
chopped fresh cilantro, to garnish
poppadoms, to serve

This warming, rich, and spicy dish is based on the traditional cooking style of Northern India, using chicken on the bone.

Slash the chicken fairly deeply at intervals with a sharp knife and place in a large bowl.

Mix the yogurt and curry paste together, then stir into the chicken, tossing to coat evenly. Cover and let marinate in the refrigerator for at least 1 hour.

Heat the oil in a large skillet. Add the onion and garlic and fry for 4–5 minutes, or until softened but not browned.

Stir in the cumin, gingerroot, and chili paste and cook gently for 1 minute.

Add the chicken pieces and fry gently, turning occasionally, for 10 minutes, or until evenly browned. Stir in any remaining marinade with the stock and almonds.

variation

If you prefer, use boneless chicken breasts instead of legs, and cut into large chunks for cooking.

Cover the skillet and simmer gently for an additional 15 minutes, or until the chicken is tender and the juices run clear when a skewer is inserted into the thickest part of the meat.

Season to taste with a little salt. Garnish the chicken with cilantro and serve with poppadoms.

cumin-spiced
apricot chicken

serves 4

15 minutes

35–40 minutes

4 large, skinless chicken leg quarters
finely grated rind of 1 lemon
salt and pepper
1¼ cups no-soak dried apricots
1 tbsp ground cumin
1 tsp ground turmeric
⅔ cup lowfat plain yogurt

1¼ cups brown rice
2 tbsp slivered hazelnuts or
    almonds, toasted
2 tbsp sunflower seeds, toasted

to serve
lemon wedges
fresh salad

Spiced chicken legs are partially boned and packed with dried apricots for an intense fruity flavor. A golden, spiced, lowfat yogurt coating keeps the chicken moist and tender.

Preheat the oven to 375°F/190°C. Remove any excess fat from the chicken legs.

Use a small sharp knife to carefully cut the flesh away from the thigh bone.

Scrape the meat away down as far as the knuckle. Grasp the thigh bone firmly and twist it to break it away from the drumstick.

Open out the boned part of the chicken and sprinkle with lemon rind and pepper. Pack the dried apricots into each piece of chicken. Fold over to enclose and secure with toothpicks.

Mix the cumin, turmeric, yogurt, and salt and pepper to taste together in a bowl, then brush this mixture over the chicken to coat evenly. Place the chicken in an ovenproof dish or roasting pan and bake in the preheated oven for 35–40 minutes, or until the chicken is tender and the juices run clear when a skewer is inserted into the thickest part of the meat.

Meanwhile, cook the rice in lightly salted boiling water until just tender, then drain well. Stir the nuts and sunflower seeds into the rice. Serve the chicken with the nutty rice, lemon wedges, and a fresh salad.

chile coconut chicken

serves 4

10 minutes

15–20 minutes

²/₃ cup hot Chicken Stock (see page 5)

1 oz/25 g coconut cream

1 tbsp corn oil

8 skinless, boneless chicken thighs, cut into long, thin strips

1 small, fresh red chile, thinly sliced

4 scallions, thinly sliced

4 tbsp smooth or crunchy peanut butter

finely grated rind and juice of 1 lime

to garnish

scallion tassels

fresh red chiles

freshly cooked rice, to serve

This tasty Thai-style dish has a classic sauce of lime, peanut, coconut, and chile.

variation

Serve jasmine rice with this spicy dish. It has a fragrant aroma that is well suited to Thai-style recipes.

Limes are used frequently in Thai cooking, particularly in conjunction with sweet flavors such as coconut or peanut. They are used in preference to lemons because they have a more acidic flavor, which lends freshness and tartness to many dishes. If limes are unavailable, you can use lemons instead.

Place the stock in a measuring cup and crumble the creamed coconut into the stock, stirring to dissolve.

Heat the oil in a large, heavy-bottomed skillet or a preheated wok. Add the chicken strips and cook, stirring, until golden.

Add the sliced red chile and the scallions to the pan and cook gently for a few minutes, stirring to mix all the ingredients.

Add the peanut butter, coconut cream, lime rind, and juice and simmer uncovered, stirring, for 5 minutes.

Serve with rice, garnished with a scallion tassel and a red chile.

Index